LSAT®
PrepTest 77
Unlocked

Exclusive Data, Analysis, & Explanations for the December 2015 LSAT

KAPLAN

PUBLISHING

New York

© 2017 by Kaplan, Inc.

Published by Kaplan Publishing, a division of Kaplan, Inc.
750 Third Avenue
New York, NY 10017

ISBN: 978-1-5062-2335-3
10 9 8 7 6 5 4 3 2 1

The Inside Story

PrepTest 77 was administered in December 2015. It challenged 29,115 test takers. What made this test so hard? Here's a breakdown of what Kaplan students who were surveyed after taking the official exam considered PrepTest 77's most difficult section.

Hardest PrepTest 77 Section as Reported by Test Takers

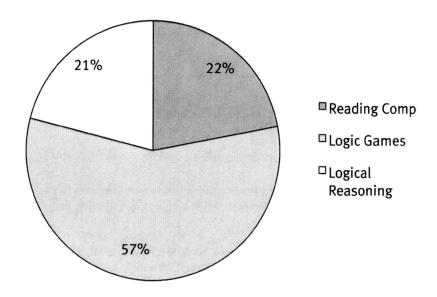

Based on these results, you might think that studying Logic Games is the key to LSAT success. Well, Logic Games is important, but test takers' perceptions don't tell the whole story. For that, you need to consider students' actual performance. The following chart shows the average number of students to miss each question in each of PrepTest 77's different sections.

Percentage Incorrect by PrepTest 77 Section Type

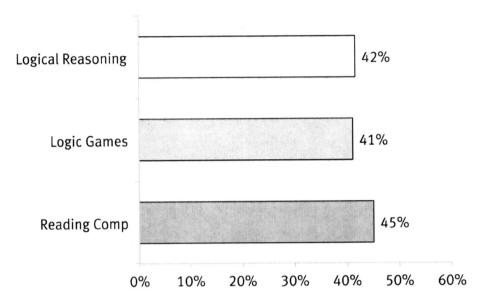

Actual student performance tells quite a different story. On average, students were almost equally likely to miss questions in all three of the different section types, and on PrepTest 77, Reading Comprehension and Logical Reasoning were somewhat higher than Logic Games in actual difficulty.

Maybe students overestimate the difficulty of the Logic Games section because it's so unusual, or maybe it's because a really hard Logic Game is so easy to remember after the test. But the truth is that the test maker places hard questions throughout the test. Here were the locations of the 10 hardest (most missed) questions in the exam.

Location of 10 Most Difficult Questions in PrepTest 77

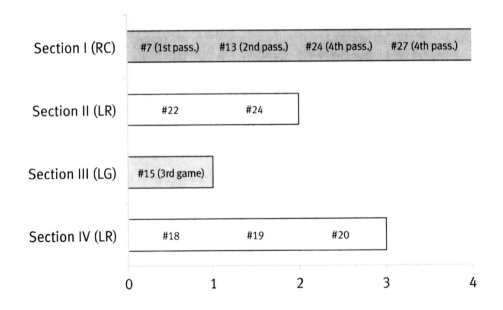

KAPLAN

The takeaway from this data is that, to maximize your potential on the LSAT, you need to take a comprehensive approach. Test yourself rigorously, and review your performance on every section of the test. Kaplan's LSAT explanations provide the expertise and insight you need to fully understand your results. The explanations are written and edited by a team of LSAT experts, who have helped thousands of students improve their scores. Kaplan always provides data-driven analysis of the test, ranking the difficulty of every question based on actual student performance. The 10 hardest questions on every test are highlighted with a 4-star difficulty rating, the highest we give. The analysis breaks down the remaining questions into 1-, 2-, and 3-star ratings so that you can compare your performance to thousands of other test takers on all LSAC material.

Don't settle for wondering whether a question was really as hard as it seemed to you. Analyze the test with real data, and learn the secrets and strategies that help top scorers master the LSAT.

7 Can't–Miss Features of PrepTest 77

- PrepTest 77 featured two Hybrid logic games—just the sixth time that had happened in a decade!
- After the test, everyone was talking about Game 3, Office Selection. Find out how LSAT experts handled this game, one unlike any other in LSAT history.
- In Logical Reasoning, PrepTest 77 featured five Role of a Statement questions. That's tied—with PrepTest 42 from December 2003—for the most ever on a single test.
- In most Logical Reasoning sections, Questions 15 to 24 are considered the Danger Zone, with the highest concentration of difficult questions. On PrepTest 77, call it the Dangr Zon, because the correct answer was never (E) on any of those questions ... in either LR section!
- PrepTest 77's Reading Comprehension section contained seven Global questions, the most since September 2006 (PT 50), which had eight.
- Who says the LSAT isn't timely? PrepTest 77 featured a passage on the punishment of white collar crime ... the same month *The Big Short* was released...
- ... and the paired passages were about feminism and gender studies, just in time for *The Hunger Games*: *Mockingjay Part 2*. There are worse tests to take, right, Katniss?

PrepTest 77 in Context

As much fun as it is to find out what makes a PrepTest unique or noteworthy, it's even more important to know just how representative it is of other LSAT administrations (and, thus, how likely it is to be representative of the exam you will face on Test Day). The following charts compare the numbers of each kind of question and game on PrepTest 77 to the average numbers seen on all officially released LSATs administered over the past five years (from 2012 through 2016).

Number of LR Questions by Type: PrepTest 77 vs. 2012–2016 Average

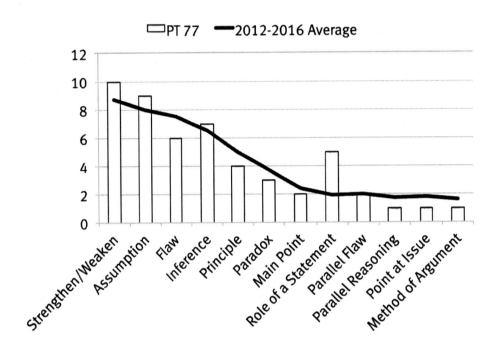

Number of LG Games by Type: PrepTest 77 vs. 2012–2016 Average

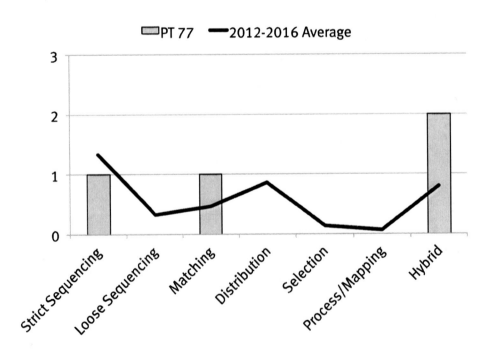

KAPLAN

Number of RC Questions by Type: PrepTest 77 vs. 2012–2016 Average

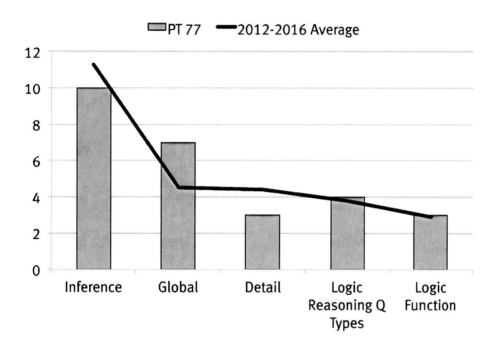

There isn't usually a huge difference in the distribution of questions from LSAT to LSAT, but if this test seems harder (or easier) to you than another you've taken, compare the number of questions of the types on which you, personally, are strongest and weakest. And then, explore within each section to see if your best or worst question types came earlier or later.

Students in Kaplan's comprehensive LSAT courses have access to every released LSAT and to an online Q-Bank with thousands of officially released questions, games, and passages. If you are studying on your own, you have to do a bit more work to identify your strengths and your areas of opportunity. Quantitative analysis (like that in the charts above) is an important tool for understanding how the test is constructed and how you are performing on it.

Section I: Reading Comprehension
Passage 1: Federal Theater Project Negro Units

Q#	Question Type	Correct	Difficulty
1	Global	C	★
2	Detail (EXCEPT)	A	★
3	Inference	C	★
4	Logic Function	D	★
5	Inference	B	★
6	Inference	E	★
7	Logic Reasoning (Strengthen)	C	★★★★

Passage 2: Corporate Crime Punishment

Q#	Question Type	Correct	Difficulty
8	Global	E	★★
9	Global	D	★
10	Inference	C	★★
11	Detail	E	★★★
12	Global	A	★
13	Inference	A	★★★★

Passage 3: Women and Gender in History

Q#	Question Type	Correct	Difficulty
14	Global	B	★
15	Inference	C	★★
16	Detail	A	★★
17	Logic Reasoning (Method of Argument)	D	★★
18	Inference	B	★★
19	Inference	E	★★★

Passage 4: Lamarckian Hereditary Mechanism

Q#	Question Type	Correct	Difficulty
20	Global	B	★★
21	Logic Function	C	★★
22	Inference	D	★
23	Global	B	★★
24	Logic Function	E	★★★★
25	Inference	B	★★★
26	Logic Reasoning (Strengthen)	A	★★★
27	Logic Reasoning (Parallel Reasoning)	E	★★★★

KAPLAN

Passage 1: Federal Theater Project Negro Units

Step 1: Read the Passage Strategically

Sample Roadmap

line #	Keyword/phrase	¶ Margin notes
3	Although	1930's
7	most important ... though	FTP
8	until recently ... little-studied	New studies "Negro Units"
14	Defying	Closest to nat'l black theater
16	overcoming	
17	arguably	
19	truly	
24	Thus	FTP introduced during creative period
28	gave rise to	Debates about content motivated by broader debates
29	vigorous ... heated ... :	Led to diverse productions
30	favored	Ex. Swing Mikado
31	preferred	
33	advocated	
36	motivated ... larger ... whether	
37	should	
39	whether it should	
41	whether it should	
42	disagreements ... resulted in	
45	Among them	
49	challenged	
52	Although	FTP short-lived, but valuable
53	provided a lifeline	
55	allowed	

Discussion

Paragraph 1 introduces a short-lived government program from the 1930s, the Federal Theater Project (FTP), that sponsored theater performances across the United States. The author then introduces the **Topic,** "Negro Units": a subset of the FTP that is now being recognized for its valuable focus on African American theater. This newfound recognition serves as the **Scope** of the passage. As will be noted throughout the passage, the author doesn't express many strong opinions. So, the **Purpose** of this passage is to merely describe the significance of the Negro Units.

Paragraph 2 gives some social context, indicating that the FTP appeared at a time of major developments in African American art. Negro Unit producers debated about what to perform. These debates were spurred by larger debates about the intended audience and the cultural impact. This led to a diverse selection of productions. The author provides an example of *The Swing Mikado*—a musical casting black people in white roles that challenges people's perspectives.

Paragraph 3 sees the end of the FTP. While it only lasted a few years, it helped save theater during the Great Depression, and the Negro Units helped African American artists bring their diverse productions to a nationwide audience. The author's **Main Idea** combines this result with the gist of the first paragraph: Negro Units are now being recognized for their ability to give African American artists a literal stage for voicing their diverse ideas.

1. (C) Global

Step 2: Identify the Question Type

This is a Global question because it asks for the "main point of the passage."

Step 3: Research the Relevant Text

Global questions are based on the entire text. Use the Main Idea as a perfect prediction here.

Step 4: Make a Prediction

The Negro Units have recently been recognized as important in helping African American artists bring their diverse beliefs to American audiences through the theater.

Step 5: Evaluate the Answer Choices

(C) correctly summarizes the recent recognition of the Negro Units' value.

(A) is Extreme and a Distortion. The Negro Units are being recognized for their legacy and contribution to African American theater, not their talent or stage performance. Further, the author states that they are "*[o]ne* of the most important" parts of the FTP, not necessarily *the* most influential.

(B) is Out of Scope. The author only cites the effect of the FTP and does not address its effect relative to any other government programs.

(D) is too narrow and not supported. Some producers favored folk dramas (lines 29–30), but there is no indication that this is what Negro Units are "best known" for—and this would hardly be the point of the whole passage.

(E) is too narrow, focusing only on details in the last paragraph about theater in general. It completely misses the author's focus on the Negro Units and their contribution to African American theater.

2. (A) Detail (EXCEPT)

Step 2: Identify the Question Type

Four answers will list what the FTP did, "[a]ccording to the passage." That means these will be details directly stated in the passage. The correct answer will not be mentioned or will distort what is actually said.

Step 3: Research the Relevant Text

The FTP in general is described in lines 1–7. Some answers are likely to be found there. The rest of paragraph 1 describes what the Negro Units did, and they are part of the FTP. That should aid with any remaining answers.

Step 4: Make a Prediction

There are many details in the first paragraph, so it's not worth predicting which ones will populate the wrong answers. Furthermore, there are an infinite number of facts that are *not* mentioned, so it's impossible to predict the correct answer. Just use details from the passage to knock out answers that are mentioned and/or look for something that clearly goes out of scope.

Step 5: Evaluate the Answer Choices

(A) is not mentioned, and is thus the correct answer. In fact, this would be impossible because the FTP "existed for only four years" (line 3).

(B) mentions operation in multiple cities, which is found in line 14.

(C) mentions the production of African American plays, which is found in line 10.

(D) mentions designers and technicians, who are listed among the employed in line 12.

(E) mentions weekly performances, as found in line 6.

3. (C) Inference

Step 2: Identify the Question Type

The correct answer will be something with which the author is "most likely to agree." That means it won't be stated directly, but it will be a valid Inference supported by the text.

Step 3: Research the Relevant Text

There are no context clues for reference, so the entire passage is relevant.

Step 4: Make a Prediction

The correct answer can be supported by anything from the text, so prediction will be impossible here. Instead, stay focused on the scope of the passage, and eliminate answers that distort or misrepresent what is said.

Step 5: Evaluate the Answer Choices

(C) is supported by lines 42–44, in which the philosophical and aesthetic debates described in paragraph 2 "resulted in a wide range of productions reflecting … diverse views."

(A) is not supported. In fact, the FTP is said to have had weekly audiences up to "half a million people" (lines 6–7). It's implied at the end that the FTP was merely in place to support theater during the Great Depression.

(B) is an unsupported comparison. There's no mention of how polarized the views of Harlem Renaissance artists were. The only polarized views described are those of the Negro Unit producers.

(D) is Out of Scope. There is no mention of today's artists, let alone their artistic contribution.

(E) is an unsupported comparison. Urban dramas and folk dramas were among the plays debated among producers (lines 29–32), but there's no indication which one was more popular.

4. (D) Logic Function

Step 2: Identify the Question Type

The phrase "in order to" at the end of the question reveals that this is asking *why* the author references the Harlem Renaissance. That makes this a Logic Function question.

Step 3: Research the Relevant Text

While the Harlem Renaissance is mentioned only in the beginning of the second paragraph, it's important to understand how that relates to what follows. Use the roadmap and margin notes for paragraph 2 for full context.

Step 4: Make a Prediction

The author mentions that the FTP followed ("came on the heels of") the Harlem Renaissance. The Keyword *Thus* (line 24) gives away the point this leads to: the FTP came along at a time when the African American community was already teeming with diverse social ideas, and it was this diverse set of beliefs that led to the debates described throughout the rest of the paragraph. So, the author mentioned the Harlem Renaissance to provide insight into what African American society was like at the time, which impacted the FTP and its Negro Units.

Step 5: Evaluate the Answer Choices

(D) correctly addresses the author's ultimate goal of providing context: the historical background that led to the subsequent debates among Negro Unit producers.

(A) is too focused on details. Yes, it was a successful artistic movement. Yes, it preceded the Negro Units, but *why* did the author mention this? That's what the question is asking for. The author has no need to just provide examples of other artistic movements. The author's focus is on what made the Negro Units so valuable, and the Harlem Renaissance is mentioned only to further that agenda.

(B) is Out of Scope. There's no mention of "overall political advancement of the African American community."

(C) is Out of Scope. The author never discusses why Negro Units "fell into obscurity."

(E) is a Faulty Use of Detail. Any relationship between African American culture and mainstream U.S. culture is only mentioned as part of the debate within Negro Units, not as part of the Harlem Renaissance.

5. (B) Inference

Step 2: Identify the Question Type

The question asks for what the author "most likely means," which indicates an Inference question. The correct answer will be supported by the text and will indicate the intended definition of "a truly national black theater."

Step 3: Research the Relevant Text

The question stem points to lines 19–20, but the entire description of the Negro Units from lines 7–20 provide a clearer picture.

Step 4: Make a Prediction

The author claims that the concept of a "national black theater" was nearly attained by the Negro Units. What they did was produce plays with African American ideas for African American audiences throughout the United States. So, the "national black theater" would be the ideal: the ultimate concept of bringing African American ideas to a nationwide audience through performing arts.

Step 5: Evaluate the Answer Choices

(B) accurately describes a large-scale artistic endeavor to spread African American ideas.

(A) equivocates with respect to the term *theater*. This answer uses *theater* to mean a physical building (a "performing arts center"), whereas the author uses *theater* to refer to the general artistic medium.

(C) distorts the government's intentions. The government was just promoting theater in general. The Negro Units promoted African American arts. Even so, that promotion actually happened. The "truly national black theater" is more of an ideal that Negro Units "came close ... to founding."

(D) is a Distortion. "Theater" refers to the full production of such plays, not just the plays themselves. Besides, there's no indication of this having to be "endorsed by scholars."

(E) also mistranslates the word *theater*. *Theater* is meant to refer to the artistic medium, not a physical "playhouse."

6. (E) Inference

Step 2: Identify the Question Type

According to the question, there will be "support for inferring" the correct answer, making this easy to spot as an Inference question.

Step 3: Research the Relevant Text

The question asks about the producers of *The Swing Mikado*, which is brought up at the end of the second paragraph (line 45). The correct answer will be consistent with the details about that play (lines 45–51). Also, the play is provided as an example of a work that sprung from the debates described earlier (lines 29–44), so those will also provide helpful context.

Step 4: Make a Prediction

The Swing Mikado is described as a musical that casts black performers in what's traditionally a "white classic." This play "challenged" audience members and their perceptions. The producers who chose such a play fit the description of those who argued for "adapting dramas written by white playwrights" (lines 33–34).

Step 5: Evaluate the Answer Choices

(E) matches the use of African American actors performing a traditionally white drama.

(A) is a 180. The play challenged audiences, which suggests that it intentionally touched on controversial ideas.

(B) is a 180. By challenging the audience to think, the producers most likely *approved* the idea of combining instruction and entertainment.

(C) is not supported. The play is merely described as a "musical," not necessarily a folk drama. Moreover, there's no mention of exploring "rural roots."

(D) is also not supported. Again, the play is merely described as a "musical," not necessarily an urban one, and there's no mention of "contemporary dilemmas."

7. (C) Logic Reasoning (Strengthen)

Step 2: Identify the Question Type

The question directly asks for something that would "strengthen" a point, making this a Strengthen question such as those found in the Logical Reasoning section.

Step 3: Research the Relevant Text

The claim in question is the author's point at the end of paragraph 1 (lines 17–20). That claim is supported by the details of the Negro Units in lines 7–14.

Step 4: Make a Prediction

The author describes a lot of Negro Unit accomplishments: defying external forces and hiring hundreds of theater folk to bring African American ideas to stages across the United States. However, there's no evidence about what happened before that. To conclude that Negro Units "came closer than any other group ... to founding a truly national black theater," the author must assume that no previous group accomplished as much toward that goal as the Negro Units. The correct answer will validate that assumption.

Step 5: Evaluate the Answer Choices

(C) helps the author's cause. If previous African American plays were exclusively produced in Eastern cities, then performing in "cities spread throughout the United States" allowed the Negro Units to be closer to "truly national" than groups that just performed on the East Coast.

(A) is a 180, suggesting that previous groups used predominantly African American ideas, just like the Negro Units.

(B) is irrelevant. Even if other projects didn't have government funding, their accomplishments could still have led to something closer to "truly national" than what the Negro Units accomplished.

(D) brings up audience size, which doesn't necessarily help the author's claim. Even if earlier groups had smaller audiences on average, those audiences could have been consistent throughout the country, allowing those groups to be more "truly national" than the Negro Units.

(E) doesn't help at all. At worst, those hard-to-find documents could potentially indicate a group that was closer than the Negro Units in establishing a "national black theater." The difficulty in finding those documents is irrelevant.

Passage 2: Corporate Crime Punishment

Step 1: Read the Passage Strategically

Sample Roadmap

line #	Keyword/phrase	¶ Margin notes
1	How severe	Punishment for corp crime?
2	e.g.	
4	? ... argue	
5	sole ... should	
6	:	Some econ. say it should just exceed profit
7	should exceed	
8	For example	
11	would feel ... justice	
12	In arguing thus ... hold	Econ: morals are irrelevant
15	such as	
17	should not	
18	argue ... should	
19	rather than	
20	But ... highly impractical ... if not	Auth: econ. proposal is impractical
21	impossible ... complicated	
22	acceptable	
23	needs to	
26	must	
27	holds ... must	
28	Otherwise	
30	even if	
32	ultimately	
34	A true reckoning ... therefore	Need to factor detection ratios
35	have to take	
36	but	
39	according to ... to be just	
40	requires	Auth: penalties too high
42	but	
44	astronomical ... necessary	
45	might arguably	
47	Thus	Need some other criterion
49	such as	
50	necessary	
51	practical ... as well as ... just	

Discussion

The passage opens with a question, which is fantastic. Opening questions usually indicate what the passage will concentrate on, and that's certainly the case here. It introduces the **Topic** (punishment for corporate crimes), and the question itself is the **Scope:** how severe should punishment for corporate crimes be? "Some economists" offer one response: the punishment should be based solely on the reckoning of cost and benefit. In other words, calculate the profit a company made through the crime, and penalize them above that value.

Paragraph 2 raises the idea that people often judge some crimes worse than others and want the more serious offenders to be more severely punished. The economists reject that, saying morals should be left out of the equation. Stick to the law and focus on offsetting profits.

In paragraph 3, the author speaks up. Starting with the Keyword *But*, the author's **Purpose** becomes clear: to refute the economists' claims. The author calls the economists' approach "impractical" and cites a complicating factor: detection ratios (i.e., the odds of getting caught). If the economists want a "true reckoning of cost and benefit" (line 34), that calculation should include the detection ratio. The example shows how this would work: if the likelihood of getting caught for a crime is 1 in 10, the penalty would be 10 times the profit (e.g., $60 million penalty for a crime that netted $6 million).

Paragraph 4 describes the potential problem. With detection ratios close to the 1-in-10 scenario as previously illustrated, penalties would be enormous. Companies would have to shut down, and people would be out of work. That leads to the author's **Main Idea:** punishment for corporate crimes should factor in criteria other than just cost and benefit reckoning to ensure penalties are both just and practical.

8. (E) Global

Step 2: Identify the Question Type

This is a Global question because it asks for the "main point of the passage."

Step 3: Research the Relevant Text

Because this is a Global question, the entire passage is relevant.

Step 4: Make a Prediction

The Main Idea from Step 1 provides an adequate prediction: corporate crime penalties should not be based solely on reckoning cost and benefit, but should consider other factors to ensure practicality.

Step 5: Evaluate the Answer Choices

(E) is correct. It addresses the impractical nature of using just cost and benefit reckoning, and suggests additional criteria as a supplement.

(A) is a Distortion. By paragraph 3, detection rates would not "supplement" the reckoning of cost and benefit; they would be included in that calculation (lines 34–35). And that approach leads to "astronomical penalties" (line 44) that are hardly practical.

(B) is a 180. When detection ratios are taken into account, that results in the "astronomical penalties" (line 44) decried by the author.

(C) is a Distortion. The author never states that economists are doing communities any "injustice," and the effect on communities is not the focus of this passage.

(D) is a Distortion. A true reckoning *would* take detection ratios into account (lines 34–35). Furthermore, the author's purpose does not involve satisfying moral standards or sending a message to corporations.

9. (D) Global

Step 2: Identify the Question Type

The question asks for the "primary purpose" of the entire passage, making this a Global question.

Step 3: Research the Relevant Text

For Global questions, the entire passage is relevant.

Step 4: Make a Prediction

The Purpose was identified as soon as the author used the Keyword *But* at the beginning of paragraph 3: to criticize the economists' approach to punishing corporate crime.

Step 5: Evaluate the Answer Choices

(D) is a perfect match.

(A) is Out of Scope. The author never addresses the courts themselves.

(B) is Out of Scope. The passage is about punishing those crimes, not describing the motives behind them.

(C) is a Faulty Use of Detail. While some communities may want to do this (as per paragraph 2), it is not the author's focus.

(E) is a Distortion. The author does advocate for a new approach, but is much more general ("some other criterion" in lines 47–48). Moral weight is offered as one example, but the author is not necessarily pushing that idea entirely.

10. (C) Inference

Step 2: Identify the Question Type

The question asks for something which the author is "most likely" to suggest, making this an Inference question.

Step 3: Research the Relevant Text

The question asks for a penalty the author might endorse for a crime with a 1-in-10 detection rate. The impact of that detection rate is described in lines 28–33. The author then outlines a general suggestion in lines 47–51 that counteracts the potential problems described in lines 43–47.

Step 4: Make a Prediction

In lines 50–51, the author wants to ensure that penalties are "practical as well as just," as opposed to what the economists propose, which would involve "astronomical penalties" and could "put convicted corporations out of business." However, by lines 28–33, if a penalty isn't big enough, companies would just take the 1-in-10 chance repeatedly, knowing that the profit made from their multiple successes will far outweigh the handful of times they get caught. So, to be practical, the author would endorse a middle ground penalty that is large enough to deter illicit behavior without causing financial ruin.

Step 5: Evaluate the Answer Choices

(C) is just the kind of middle ground the author would support.

(A) is too small a penalty to be practical. Companies would gladly give up that profit knowing that they could just commit the crime again and keep the profit when they *don't* get caught.

(B) is also too small to be practical. Companies would still be willing to risk committing further crimes "even if the potential penalty is somewhat larger than the profit" (lines 30–31).

(D) is a 180. This would be the kind of "astronomical penalty" the author argues against.

(E) is a 180. This is exactly the kind of scenario the author wants to avoid.

11. (E) Detail

Step 2: Identify the Question Type

The question asks for a view that the author "ascribes" to the economists. That means it will be stated directly in the passage, making this a Detail question.

Step 3: Research the Relevant Text

A quick glance indicates that each answer refers to "a community's moral judgment." The economist's view of that is presented in paragraph 2.

Step 4: Make a Prediction

According to the economists, a community's moral judgment "should not be a factor in determining penalties" (line 17).

Step 5: Evaluate the Answer Choices

(E) matches the economists' view about disregarding the community's judgment when calculating penalties.

(A) is Out of Scope. The economists make no claim about the reliability of the community's judgment.

(B) is a 180. The economists outright claim that judgments *should not* be a factor, not even "occasionally."

(C) may be the case, but the economists never express that point of view.

(D) is a Distortion. The community's judgment may be irrelevant to assessing the *penalty* for the crime, but could still be relevant to determining a company's morality. However, the economists are not interested in determining a company's morality.

12. (A) Global

Step 2: Identify the Question Type

This question asks for the "organization of the passage" in its entirety. That makes this a Global question.

Step 3: Research the Relevant Text

The organization of the passage should be outlined clearly in the margin notes.

Step 4: Make a Prediction

Consider the purpose of each paragraph in order. Paragraph 1 poses a question and provides one answer (the economists' proposal). Paragraph 2 discusses one factor involved in that response (the role of morality). Paragraph 3 introduces a complication (detection ratio). Paragraph 4 describes the consequence and pushes for an alternative solution. The correct answer should hit these major points in order.

Step 5: Evaluate the Answer Choices

(A) is a perfect rundown from top to bottom.

(B) is perfect until the very end. The author does raise a criticism (the detection ratio), but the author does not reject that criticism. The criticism is accepted and spurs the author's call for an alternate solution.

(C) distorts the passage by focusing too much on the "ethics of [the economists]." The author has nothing against their ethics. The problem is in the application of the detection ratio.

(D) goes astray by mentioning two answers that are identified and compared. The author only raises one answer to the initial question and then rejects it. If there's a second answer, it's the author proposal at the very end, but the author never compares it to anything or identifies any assumption underlying it.

(E) goes Out of Scope quickly by mentioning the "consequences of failing to solve the problem."

13. (A) Inference

Step 2: Identify the Question Type

This is an Inference question because it asks for something with which the economists are "most likely to agree."

Step 3: Research the Relevant Text

Be careful. The question asks about the economists' point of view, not the author's. Be sure to use the economists' arguments as presented in paragraphs 1 and 2.

Step 4: Make a Prediction

There's a lot of text, so don't predict an exact answer. Instead, start by testing the answers against a general summary of the economists' proposal: penalize companies based on the reckoning of cost and benefit (paragraph 1), and only worry about affecting earnings rather than assessing morality (paragraph 2). If needed, go back to those paragraphs to confirm support for any answer that seems plausible.

Step 5: Evaluate the Answer Choices

(A) is correct. By lines 17–19, all that matters is that the law affects earnings. As further support, the author claims that following the economists' "reckoning of cost and benefit only" plan could put corporations out of business, suggesting that this is not a concern for the economists.

(B) is a Distortion. The community's opinion should be a factor in determining the *penalty*, but could still be a factor in assigning moral weight. However, the economists have no concern with assigning moral weight.

(C) would be correct if it stopped before the word *unless*. However, that *unless* suggests a possible exception when it would be okay to consider moral offensiveness. The economists do not allow for such exceptions.

(D) is Extreme and a Distortion. The detection ratio that should be involved is about the likelihood of being caught for a crime, not the likelihood of "recommitting" the crime. Furthermore, even if this answer did get the definition of detection ratio right, there's no indication that it's the "main factor" in calculating penalties.

(E) is Out of Scope. The economists' proposal is simply based on the reckoning of cost and benefit. There's no mention in their proposal of factoring in prior convictions.

Passage 3: Women and Gender in History

Step 1: Read the Passage Strategically

Sample Roadmap

line #	Keyword/phrase	¶ Margin notes
Passage A		
2	both … dramatic	1990's
3	and	in history, shift from studying individual women to general gender issues
10	seemed … retreat	
12	:	
18	but … also reveals	Studying "women" too narrow
19	so often dismissed … too	
24–26		Studying "gender" allows greater emphasis
27	And yet … lost	Auth: focus on gender
28	share the suspicion	obscures individual
29	obscure … as …	accomplishments
30	much as … reveals	
31	overlook	
Passage B		
35	promote	Aug.'s laws promote family
37	resting upon	
38	particular …	Defined women as domestic
39	attention	
44	thereby	Good women = good state
45	particular …	
46	attention	
47	:	
48	Thus	
49	more	Values of women recognized but restricted
50	but also more	
52	became clear	
53	unusual	
55	should	
58		Art reflected domestic vision of women
61		

Discussion

According to passage A, women's history (**Topic**) became more mainstream in the 1990s, but with less focus on specific women and more focus on generic studies of gender relations. Instead of revealing individual accomplishments, articles discussed the cultural role of broader ideas like masculinity and domesticity. This shift toward gender issues is the **Scope**.

In paragraph 2, the author explains how just studying women can be seen as merely "celebratory," a way to remember who those women were. Nevertheless, "gender" studies can help analyze social and political structures. By paragraph 3, the author is questioning the value of this shift (**Purpose**), claiming that this focus on gender issues can cause us to overlook the effect certain individual woman had on the world (**Main Idea**).

Passage B starts off discussing emperor Augustus's desire to bring back good old-fashioned morality to Rome after the Triumviral Wars (over 2,000 years ago). He did so by passing laws promoting family. These laws (**Topic**) encouraged women to perform domestic roles as mothers and wives.

Paragraph 2 further discusses the role women played in these laws (**Scope**). Augustus viewed women as integral to his plan. Simply put, if women just stayed home and were good mothers and wives, there would be peace and prosperity in Rome. This gave women more visibility, but restricted them to those domestic roles. Paragraph 3 describes how art of that era expressed this supposedly "idealized" world created by Augustus. The author here expresses no opinion, so the **Purpose** is merely to describe the situation. The **Main Idea** is that Augustus's laws encouraged women to take on domestic roles in order to ensure political stability in Rome.

14. (B) Global

Step 2: Identify the Question Type

The question asks for the "central topic" of each passage, making this a Global question.

Step 3: Research the Relevant Text

All of the text is relevant to this question. Instead, focus on the Main Idea of each passage, as discovered in Step 1.

Step 4: Make a Prediction

Passage A is focused on the study of gender roles and how it allows for analysis of social and political structures. Passage B is focused on a specific sociopolitical event in history, but one that focuses on the role of women in that event. So, the central idea of both passages revolves around gender issues in a social and political context.

Step 5: Evaluate the Answer Choices

(B) is correct.

(A) mentions a decline in studying individual women, which is only addressed in passage A.

(C) mentions ancient Rome, which is only discussed in passage B.

(D) mentions the role of masculinity, which is only brought up in passage A (and hardly the central topic).

(E) mentions the "celebratory" goals of women's history, a concept only broached in passage A.

15. (C) Inference

Step 2: Identify the Question Type

The question asks for something with which the author of passage A is "most likely to agree." That makes this an Inference question.

Step 3: Research the Relevant Text

The question is too vague to suggest any particular reference point in the passages. Instead, use the general ideas and the roadmap to get a sense of the correct answer.

Step 4: Make a Prediction

The author of passage A expresses the strongest opinions in paragraph 3, suspecting that analysis of gender roles "obscures" the "ways in which individual women engaged their worlds." The analysis in passage B matches that suspicion by describing the general role of women under Augustus's laws without providing any information about individual women.

Step 5: Evaluate the Answer Choices

(C) accurately matches the analysis in passage B to the description in passage A.

(A) is not supported. No comparison is made between the gender roles described in passage B and those in modern times.

(B) is a Distortion. The analysis in passage B focuses more on women's domestic role than it does on "femininity" per se. Even if it did focus on femininity, the author of passage A never suggests that studying masculinity is equally important.

(D) is not supported. There is no information in either passage about the role of domesticity in recent politics.

(E) is Out of Scope. There's no suggestion that historians were unaware of any of these laws.

16. (A) Detail

Step 2: Identify the Question Type

"According to" the passage typically indicates a Detail question, and the language is strong enough here (e.g., it's not asking for something *suggested* or *implied*) to indicate that the correct answer will be directly stated.

Step 3: Research the Relevant Text

The shift that happened in the 1990s is described at the very beginning of passage A. Note that the question asks for what the focus shifted *to*, so don't worry about what it shifted away *from*.

Step 4: Make a Prediction

The opening sentence mentions the transition "to the issue of gender issues" (line 4). In the subsequent lines, this is said to involve "turning to an exploration of the social systems that underlay the relationships of men and women" (lines 7–9).

Step 5: Evaluate the Answer Choices

(A) matches the verbiage of lines 7–9 practically word for word.

(B) is a Distortion. There's no suggestion that gender studies are "bringing attention" to something "previously ignored." If anything, this better fits the kind of women's studies people are moving away from, as described in lines 23–24 (finding lost ancestors and restoring them in our memories).

(C) is a Distortion. The author never mentions gender bias affecting traditional scholarship.

(D) is Out of Scope. There is no criticism of earlier historians.

(E) is a Distortion. While some specific articles might focus on domesticity, that's not the general focus in studying women's history. Also, there's no mention of "documenting shifts in the conception of domesticity."

17. (D) Logic Reasoning (Method of Argument)

Step 2: Identify the Question Type

The question asks for the "relationship" between both passages. The answers will describe *how* the authors present their material and *how* they relate. Finding *how* arguments proceed is the hallmark of a Method of Argument question.

Step 3: Research the Relevant Text

The question refers to the passages as a whole, so there's no particular reference point for research.

Step 4: Make a Prediction

Passage A is a general discussion of the shift toward gender studies in history. Passage B describes the laws of Augustus, a specific event that illustrates the shift described in passage A. The correct answer should address this connection.

Step 5: Evaluate the Answer Choices

(D) is a match. The "trend in scholarship" is the shift toward gender studies. Passage A does indicate some strengths (paragraph 2) and weaknesses (paragraph 3), and the study in passage B is a perfect example of that trend.

(A) is a 180. The author of passage A is suspicious of the trend and complains that it "obscures as much as it reveals." That's hardly an endorsement.

(B) falls apart because passage A never addresses passage B directly. Besides, there's no mention of overlooked evidence.

(C) doesn't work because, while the evidence in passage B is consistent with what's described in passage A, they have different goals in their conclusions. Passage A expresses opinions about fairly recent trends, while passage B is more of a factual account of ancient events.

(E) is off because there's no argument in passage B for passage A to advance.

18. (B) Inference

Step 2: Identify the Question Type

This question asks for something in passage A that "most closely" corresponds to something in passage B. That makes this an Inference question.

Step 3: Research the Relevant Text

Start by analyzing the provided lines for passage B. Then, use content clues in that text to search for matching ideas in passage A.

Step 4: Make a Prediction

The question provides a reference to lines 36–43, which describe laws allocating "domestic" roles to women to help preserve "peace and stability" to Rome. This lines up nicely with the articles described in lines 14–16 about how "domesticity ... shaped culture and politics."

Step 5: Evaluate the Answer Choices

(B) matches the wording from passage A that corresponds to the details referenced in passage B.

(A) is a 180. The "history of women per se" is what historians are said to "retreat from" (lines 10–11). That would be a focus on women as individuals, which is not what passage B entails.

(C) is a 180. Rediscovering and honoring lost ancestors is part of the "celebratory" study of women's history (lines 21–24), which focuses on individual women. Nothing in passage B does that.

(D) is Out of Scope. There's nothing in the lines of passage B that discusses the role of masculinity.

(E) a Distortion. There's nothing in the passage B lines referenced that suggests that anything was obscured.

19. (E) Inference

Step 2: Identify the Question Type

This is an Inference question because it asks for something with which the author of passage A is "most likely to agree."

Step 3: Research the Relevant Text

There are no content clues, so all of the text is relevant.

Step 4: Make a Prediction

Passage B describes details of the laws passed in ancient Rome by Augustus. It matches the kind of scholarship described throughout passage A in that it focuses on general gender issues instead of the role of any women in particular. However, despite concerns about aspects being overlooked (paragraph 3), the author of passage A does concede that analyses like that of passage B can "offer an analytic framework within which to analyze social and political structures."

Step 5: Evaluate the Answer Choices

(E) is supported in that the details of passage B do provide insight into Roman politics and culture, an advantage that passage A does admit exists.

(A) is Out of Scope. The author of passage A never discusses the integration of women's history as being "far from complete."

(B) is a 180. The author of passage A is suspicious of abandoning such efforts and would hardly claim such actions to be "justified."

(C) is a Distortion. Passage B does illustrate the current trend, but that trend is toward gender studies, not a specific focus on women's political influence.

(D) is a 180. Gender roles are the focus of recent studies and *are* seen as significant.

Passage 4: Lamarckian Hereditary Mechanism

Step 1: Read the Passage Strategically

Sample Roadmap

line #	Keyword/phrase	¶ Margin notes
4	basic idea	Lamarck: organisms adapt, pass to offspring
7	ridiculed	
8	for example	
11	adamant	Most bio. disagree
12	But	
13	attempting to revive	Steele: evidence in immune system
14	claim ... evidence	
18	:	How does immune system work?
23	unusual	
24	most common	DNA → RNA, mutates
27		immune system finds defense
29		
30	hypothesizes	Steele: RNA → DNA
31	Indeed	
33	But	
34	troublesome question ... :	New DNA to reprod system?
38	? ... believe this is possible	
39	elegant ... but speculative	Steele: Yes, via virus
44	But ... even if	actually happen?
45	?	
47	we must make do	
48	claim	Steele offers circumstantial evidence
51	claim	
55	not so	Some bio, still not convinced
56	easily swayed ... suggest ... less ...	
57	radical	

Discussion

Paragraph 1 opens by introducing the **Topic**: the evolutionary theory of Jean-Baptiste de Lamarck. Lamarck suggested that animals adapt to their environment and pass those adaptations on to their offspring. While most biologists dismiss Lamarck's theory, one scientist claims to have found supporting evidence involving the immune system. This attempt at confirming Lamarck's theory is the **Scope** of the passage.

Before getting to Steele's ideas, paragraph 2 provides some background on immune systems. Immune systems help defend against diseases, in part, through mutation. When DNA is copied over to RNA, some immune system cells mutate—a process described as a genetic "typo." The immune system finds out which mutation works, which then helps the body defend itself.

Paragraph 3 introduces Steele's belief that this altered RNA will turn back into DNA, a general process that has been observed previously. However, the author raises the question of whether this new DNA could replace the DNA in the reproductive system and thus be passed on to offspring. Steele believes so, suggesting that the new DNA could be brought to the reproductive system by a virus.

The author raises more questions in paragraph 4, most importantly: does this actually happen? It's never been seen, but Steele insists that he and his team have found evidence. He claims reproductive genes have a "signature" with instructions for the immune system. Mutations to those genes would indicate that information was indeed transferred from somewhere else. Despite this evidence, some biologists are not convinced.

The author raises a lot of questions, but the focus remains on Steele's theories. So, the author's **Purpose** is to merely inform the reader. The **Main Idea** is that Steele and his team claim to have evidence supporting Lamarck's theory that genetic adaptations can be passed along to offspring.

20. (B) Global

Step 2: Identify the Question Type

The question asks for the "main point" of the passage, making this a Global question.

Step 3: Research the Relevant Text

For Global questions, there's no need to go back into the passage. The Main Idea from Step 1 will be enough here.

Step 4: Make a Prediction

Stay neutral with this. Steele and his team claim to have found evidence supporting Lamarck's theory that genetic adaptations can be passed along to offspring.

Step 5: Evaluate the Answer Choices

(B) matches, citing Steele's evidence for a Lamarckian system that would pass along genetic characteristics.

(A) is Extreme. Steele claims to have found evidence, but the lackluster response of biologists shows that he hasn't quite "proven" anything yet.

(C) goes against what's said in paragraph 3, which claims that Steele "believes" changes can be passed along to offspring, but this is merely "speculative." That doesn't suggest that he succeeded.

(D) is a Distortion. The author never compares Steele's work to the standard theory of evolution, and the tone of this answer is too negative for what's really a more neutral passage.

(E) is a Distortion on many fronts. RNA reverting back to DNA had already been "observed frequently" (line 33), and there's no suggestion that this was the "main obstacle" to accepting Lamarck's theory. Furthermore, by the end, Lamarck's theory is *still* not generally accepted.

21. (C) Logic Function

Step 2: Identify the Question Type

The phrase "primarily in order to" indicates a Logic Function question. The question is asking *why* the author refers to a mutation as a "typo."

Step 3: Research the Relevant Text

The term "typo" appears in line 25, but be sure to read the entire sentence from 24–27 for context.

Step 4: Make a Prediction

"Typo" refers to a mutation that occurs when DNA is "transcribed" (i.e., copied) into RNA. In other words, when a DNA strand is copied, a change occurs that is akin to a typo—a slight error in the copy that results in something a little different.

Step 5: Evaluate the Answer Choices

(C) correctly expresses the concept of a minor error copying one thing to another.

(A) is a 180 because these mutations *are* adaptive—changing to help the body defend itself.

(B) is a 180. The mutation is *very* consequential, helping the body defend itself against diseases.

(D) is Out of Scope. There's no suggestion that this change is easily overlooked.

(E) is a clever Distortion. The analogy to a text-based "typo" makes it easier to understand what's happening. However, the author's intention is to clarify what the mutation is like. The author does not compare scientific analysis and textual analysis.

22. (D) Inference

Step 2: Identify the Question Type

The question asks for the author's attitude, which the passage "strongly suggests." That's the sign of an Inference question.

Step 3: Research the Relevant Text

Steele's theory is described throughout paragraphs 3 and 4. Look for Keywords indicating the author's voice throughout those paragraphs.

Step 4: Make a Prediction

The author doesn't express any views directly about Steele's theory. The author does raise many questions, but Steele always has an answer. However, it is telling that the author keeps noting that Steele merely "hypothesizes" (line 30) about things he and his team "believe" (lines 38 and 41). The author even qualifies one claim as "speculative" (line 39). While the author doesn't outright dismiss Steele's theory, the author is much more in sync with the biologists who are "not so easily swayed" (lines 55–56).

Step 5: Evaluate the Answer Choices

(D) fits the author's constant questioning and refusal to admit Steele's theories as anything more than just beliefs.

(A) is a 180. With so many questions, the author seems hardly confident that Steele is correct.

(B) is not supported. The author doesn't express any ill feelings toward Steele and never professes any allegiance to Darwinism.

(C) is a Distortion. The author does seem to have trust issues, but they have nothing to do with the "novelty" of the theory.

(E) is not supported. Steele has answers to every question posed, which suggests plenty of rigor on his part. The author holds no grudge against Steele for being lazy.

23. (B) Global

Step 2: Identify the Question Type

The question asks what the passage is "primarily concerned with," making this a Global question.

Step 3: Research the Relevant Text

With Global questions, there's no need to go back to the text. For this question, just consider the author's Purpose as determined in Step 1.

Step 4: Make a Prediction

The author's purpose for the passage is merely to introduce Steele's theory and the evidence he supplies for that theory.

Step 5: Evaluate the Answer Choices

(B) gets it right. The author is merely describing Steele's attempt to support Lamarck's much-ridiculed theory of evolution.

(A) is a Distortion. The passage describes a modern attempt to support the theory, not the development of that theory in the first place.

(C) is too narrow. A series of questions about the immune system is raised in paragraph 2, but the rest of the passage moves past that into reproductive systems and passing genes on to offspring.

(D) is a Distortion. While Steele and his team may feel the theory has merits, the author is not concerned with evaluating those merits. The author is only concerned with Steele's findings.

(E) is Out of Scope. The author is only focused on Lamarck's theory, not on the philosophy of science in general.

24. (E) Logic Function

Step 2: Identify the Question Type

The question directly asks for the function of the last paragraph.

Step 3: Research the Relevant Text

Use the margin notes for paragraph 4, and be sure to determine how that relates to the previous paragraphs.

Step 4: Make a Prediction

The bulk of the last paragraph describes the "circumstantial evidence" that Steel provides to support the theory he argues for earlier in the passage.

Step 5: Evaluate the Answer Choices

(E) correctly identifies the discussion of evidence to support Steele's neo-Lamarckian theory (i.e., the theory meant to revive Lamarckism).

(A) is a Distortion. While the last paragraph states that some biologists are not entirely swayed, it doesn't present "various objections" to Steele's theory.

(B) is a 180. Steele *does* provide supporting evidence, even if that evidence hasn't been generally accepted.

(C) is Out of Scope. The author offers no revision to Steele's theory.

(D) is Out of Scope. The author offers no suggestions for further research.

25. (B) Inference

Step 2: Identify the Question Type

This question asks for something the passage "suggests" that the author would "agree with." That makes this an Inference question.

Step 3: Research the Relevant Text

There are no context clues here, so the entire passage is relevant.

Step 4: Make a Prediction

With no hints in the question stem, the correct answer could reference anything from anywhere in the passage. In this case, go through the answers one at a time, eliminating those that are clearly wrong. Then, use content clues in the remaining answers to do any necessary research.

Step 5: Evaluate the Answer Choices

(B) is supported by paragraph 3. While reverse transcription has been observed frequently "in other contexts," the author states that Steele merely "hypothesizes" that immune cell RNA would do it, too. That suggests he hasn't actually observed it happening yet.

(A) is not supported. The author never suggests that the doubting biologists are mistaken.

(C) takes a lot of details and mixes them up improperly. Lines 41–43 suggest that viruses carry DNA that has *already been altered*. The virus itself does not alter the DNA.

(D) is a 180. As Steele's theory is described, the passing along of characteristics takes place when DNA is transferred out of the immune system and into the reproductive system.

(E) is Extreme. While Steele's theory may still be considered "speculative," the author never suggests that direct observation is the key to moving a theory from speculation to science.

26. (A) Logic Reasoning (Strengthen)

Step 2: Identify the Question Type

The question directly asks for something that would strengthen Steele's position. Treat this question as it would be treated in Logical Reasoning.

Step 3: Research the Relevant Text

Steele's position is laid out in paragraph 4, with evidence provided in paragraph 3.

Step 4: Make a Prediction

The gist of Steele's theory is that the DNA that's altered in the immune system is transferred to the reproductive system by a virus (lines 41–43). However, Steele has never seen this happen and only has circumstantial evidence. If there were actual evidence of DNA being transported by a virus, that would help Steele out.

Step 5: Evaluate the Answer Choices

(A) helps greatly. If a virus was shown to bring new DNA into reproductive cells and make a change, then Steele would have something more than mere conjecture.

(B) is a 180. Steele says that the appearance of such patterns in reproductive genes suggests a transfer from the immune system (lines 51–55). If those patterns are also found in nervous system genes, it's possible the patterns are found everywhere and may not have been transferred from one place to another.

(C) adds nothing to Steele's argument. The way this process is described—the immune system will "test out different defenses until it finds one that does the job" (lines 27–29)—already appears to be random trial and error. This doesn't help Steele's claim that mutations are then transferred by a virus.

(D) is a Faulty Use of Detail, supporting Lamarck's supposed presumption in lines 8–10. However, this does not support *Steele's* theory about passing along immune system mutations to offspring.

(E) discusses "acquired immunities" as opposed to those that developed through genetic mutation. So, that doesn't help Steele out.

27. (E) Logic Reasoning (Parallel Reasoning)

Step 2: Identify the Question Type

The correct answer asks for evidence "analogous to" that described in the last paragraph. That makes this a Parallel Reasoning question.

Step 3: Research the Relevant Text

The evidence in the last paragraph is described in lines 48–55.

Step 4: Make a Prediction

The question stem presents a situation with a copy of an ancient text. One scholar hypothesizes that the text isn't wholly original and was changed by a copyist at some point. This would be similar to Steele finding DNA in the reproductive system and hypothesizing that it's not original DNA and it was changed at some point. Steele's evidence in the last paragraph involves a "distinct pattern of mutations" that doesn't match the standard "signature" of reproductive cells. To complete the analogy in the question stem, the scholar should have evidence of "distinct" changes that don't match the "signature" style of the original era.

Step 5: Evaluate the Answer Choices

(E) fits the analogy. This is evidence of "distinct" changes that don't match a previous style.

(A) does not match. This offers no evidence that the changes were "distinct" to a later era.

(B) does not match. Even if there was admittance of a change, that's not parallel to finding "distinct" changes.

(C) does not match. This doesn't provide evidence of changes "distinct" to a particular era.

(D) doesn't match. This definitely indicates changes, but doesn't have any "distinct" pattern to parallel the evidence in paragraph 4.

Section II: Logical Reasoning

Q#	Question Type	Correct	Difficulty
1	Strengthen	C	★
2	Strengthen	D	★
3	Assumption (Necessary)	E	★★
4	Weaken	A	★
5	Parallel Flaw	A	★
6	Assumption (Necessary)	D	★
7	Strengthen	E	★★
8	Principle (Identify/Strengthen)	A	★
9	Assumption (Sufficient)	B	★★
10	Strengthen/Weaken (Evaluate the Argument)	C	★
11	Main Point	B	★★
12	Principle (Parallel)	B	★
13	Inference	B	★
14	Flaw	A	★★
15	Assumption (Sufficient)	C	★★
16	Principle (Identify/Strengthen)	B	★★★
17	Method of Argument	B	★★★
18	Flaw	D	★★
19	Paradox	B	★★★
20	Role of a Statement	B	★★★
21	Strengthen	A	★
22	Flaw	A	★★★★
23	Inference	D	★★
24	Assumption (Necessary)	A	★★★★
25	Inference (EXCEPT)	D	★★

1. (C) Strengthen

Step 1: Identify the Question Type

The question asks for something that will "justify" or strengthen the environmentalists' point. Look for the conclusion and any evidence, and find an answer that makes the connection more logically sound.

Step 2: Untangle the Stimulus

An electric utility is weighing two options for a new power plant: natural gas–fired or waste-to-energy. The environmentalists recommend the waste-to-energy plant, despite the fact that it produces more pollution than a gas-fired plant.

Step 3: Make a Prediction

In a way, this works very much like a Paradox question. Why would the environmentalists push an option that is liable to be worse for the environment? As with any recommendation, there are always overlooked advantages or disadvantages to consider. In this case, the environmentalist must know of some benefit to waste-to-energy plants or some problem with gas-fired plants that hasn't been mentioned. The correct answer will fill in one of those missing gaps.

Step 4: Evaluate the Answer Choices

(C) provides a resolution. Even if the waste-to-energy plant isn't quite as efficient as the gas-fired plant, it's still a much better solution than keeping what's currently available. While it may not *completely* justify the choice over the gas-fired plant, it *helps* push things in the right direction—and that's all the question asks for.

(A) is a 180. This just makes gas-fired plants seem like a better option, making it less understandable why the environmentalists would choose the waste-to-energy plant.

(B) is irrelevant. This does nothing to justify the choice of one plant over another.

(D) is a 180. If air pollution is the most serious problem, then they seem *less* justified choosing the option that will produce more air pollution.

(E) is irrelevant. Even if power plants contribute relatively little to air pollution overall, that doesn't help justify choosing the higher-polluting option.

2. (D) Strengthen

Step 1: Identify the Question Type

The question directly asks for something that strengthens the given argument. Find the evidence and conclusion, and look for an answer that validates the assumption between them.

Step 2: Untangle the Stimulus

The anthropologist concludes that cooking allows us to get the calories we need to support our large brains. "After all"

(which indicates evidence), we developed big brains when we started to control fire, and people don't get enough calories from eating just raw food.

Step 3: Make a Prediction

The evidence provides information about people who eat raw food and what happened when our ancestors controlled fire. However, the conclusion is about *cooking* food, which is never directly addressed in the evidence. The anthropologist assumes that there's something distinct about cooking food that helps us get the calories we need. The correct answer will provide a needed distinction.

Step 4: Evaluate the Answer Choices

(D) supports the anthropologist by providing something distinct about cooking food that allows us to get more calories.

(A) is a 180. If cooked foods and raw foods had the same number of calories, then cooking would do nothing to gain us more calories.

(B) is an Irrelevant Comparison. The argument is about raw vs. cooked food, not meat vs. vegetables.

(C) is a 180. If the body gets the same amount of calories from food no matter what, then cooked food offers no advantage and does nothing to give us the extra calories we need.

(E) is an Irrelevant Comparison. The argument is about cooking the food, regardless of whether it's domesticated or wild.

3. (E) Assumption (Necessary)

Step 1: Identify the Question Type

The question directly asks for an assumption, and one that is "required by the argument." That makes this a Necessary Assumption question.

Step 2: Untangle the Stimulus

Commercial honeybees face a lot of problems, but the author argues there's a root cause for all of these problems: inbreeding. The evidence is that inbreeding has reduced the bees' genetic diversity.

Step 3: Make a Prediction

What does genetic diversity have to do with these problems? For the author's argument to make any sense, there must be *some* connection between genetic diversity and the host of problems described.

Step 4: Evaluate the Answer Choices

(E) makes the necessary connection. After all, using the Denial Test, if a lack of diversity did *not* make honeybees more vulnerable, then the reduced diversity that stems from inbreeding would be irrelevant, making the whole argument fall apart.

(A) is an Irrelevant Comparison. The relative likelihood of inbreeding does nothing to connect it to the problems the commercial bees face.

(B) is irrelevant. Even if inbreeding practices *could* be undone, there's still no evidence that inbreeding is truly the cause of all the problems.

(C) is irrelevant. Whether the diversity is still dropping or has leveled out, there's still no evidence that limited diversity is really the cause of the problems.

(D) is a 180. This suggests that problems would occur regardless of how diverse the population is. That would make inbreeding *less* likely to be the root cause.

4. (A) Weaken

Step 1: Identify the Question Type

The question outright asks for something that will weaken the given argument. Find an answer that attacks the assumption between the evidence and conclusion.

Step 2: Untangle the Stimulus

The argument starts off with some statistical information: the northern cardinal was hardly seen in Nova Scotia in 1980. Twenty years later, they became a common sight. Because winters warmed up a little during those 20 years, the author argues that those warmer temps are responsible for the sudden increase in cardinals.

Step 3: Make a Prediction

The phrase "responsible for" indicates a causal argument. In this case, the author is taking evidence of a correlation (more cardinals appeared during the same time temperatures rose) and concluding that one thing caused the other (higher temps *caused* the increase in cardinals). The most common way to weaken such an argument is to find an alternate cause, for instance some other reason the cardinals are suddenly more prevalent.

Step 4: Evaluate the Answer Choices

(A) provides an alternative explanation. The birds aren't there more for the warmer weather. They're coming for the food!

(B) is irrelevant. What matters is why they were spotted more in 2000 than in 1980. No matter how easy the bird is to spot, the author can still say weather impacted the population increase.

(C) is irrelevant. If other songbirds are also more common, the author could claim that warm weather was responsible for their increased numbers, too.

(D) just says that populations of nonmigratory birds (such as the cardinal) fluctuated more than other birds. But what caused that fluctuation? It could have been warmer weather, thus confirming the author's view.

(E) is a 180. If there were *fewer* predators in the area, *that* would weaken the argument, suggesting that the increased cardinal population was due to a threat being removed. *More* predators suggests that the cardinals are moving to Nova Scotia regardless for some other reason—perhaps because of the warmer weather.

5. (A) Parallel Flaw

Step 1: Identify the Question Type

The question asks for an argument "parallel in its reasoning" to the argument given. Moreover, the given argument is described as "flawed." That makes this a Parallel Flaw question. Identify the error in the stimulus, and look for an answer that commits the exact same error.

Step 2: Untangle the Stimulus

The author cites a connection between personality and genes. The author then concludes that personalities don't change because genes don't change.

Step 3: Make a Prediction

While personality is linked to genes, it may also be linked to other things. So, even if genes don't change, something else could change that would affect personality. The correct answer will commit this same flaw: concluding that one thing won't change (personality) because it's connected to something else that doesn't change (genes), overlooking other factors that could induce change (e.g., personal relationships).

Step 4: Evaluate the Answer Choices

(A) matches piece by piece. The author concludes that one thing won't change (understanding of WWI) because it's connected to something else that doesn't change (what happened in the war), overlooking other factors that could induce change (e.g., the discovery of missing documents).

(B) is the opposite logic, claiming that two things are connected but saying that changing one *could* change the other.

(C) tries to tempt people by sticking to the same topic (genes). However, the logic here is about actively stopping something rather than something changing. That's not the same.

(D) makes a shift between long-term effects and short-term effects, concepts not involved in the original argument.

(E) is a 180. This makes a connection between two things, but concludes that if one thing *does* change, then the other thing *changes* as well.

6. (D) Assumption (Necessary)

Step 1: Identify the Question Type

The question asks for the assumption on which the argument "depends," making this a Necessary Assumption question.

Step 2: Untangle the Stimulus

After some political brouhaha, former PM Brooks has been released from prison and is now willing to join the government of dictator McFarlane. The problem is that McFarlane's supporters don't like Brooks, and McFarlane's opponents won't support anyone in his government. So, the analyst concludes that Brooks won't get a lot of supporters.

Step 3: Make a Prediction

It is clear that Brooks is not going to get support from anyone who supports or opposes McFarlane. However, those are two extremes. What about people in the middle who don't really have a strong opinion about McFarlane? Maybe Brooks could drum up lots of support from those people. The analyst is convinced otherwise, so the analyst must assume this can't happen—that there just aren't enough people who are ambivalent about McFarlane.

Step 4: Evaluate the Answer Choices

(D) must be true. If most people *didn't* have one of these opinions, then there would be plenty of potential supporters of Brooks. The analyst must assume that most people *will* have an opinion.

(A) is irrelevant. The legitimacy of McFarlane's government has no bearing on how many supporters Brooks has.

(B) is irrelevant. Even if there *was* more corruption now than during Brooks's reign, people could *still* be unhappy with Brooks.

(C) is irrelevant. The author's argument is based on people's alignment with McFarlane, regardless of how much or how little Brooks's views overlap.

(E) is irrelevant. Whether the charges are valid or not, Brooks still seems to be out of favor with a lot of folks.

7. (E) Strengthen

Step 1: Identify the Question Type

The question directly asks for something that Strengthens the given argument.

Step 2: Untangle the Stimulus

Because amber is more valuable when it contains fossilized life, forgers will add normal-looking insects to their fake amber to drive up prices. *Therefore*, the author concludes that amber pieces with normal-looking insects are likely to be fake.

Step 3: Make a Prediction

The author reversed the logic! By the evidence, if amber is faked, forgers will add normal-looking insects:

If	*fake*	→	*normal insect*

The author concludes that if there's a normal-looking insect, it's likely to be fake:

If	*normal insect*	→	*fake*

That's not proper logic. While forgers are likely to put normal insects in their fake amber, normal insects could appear in real amber, too. The author assumes otherwise, likely believing that real amber would contain something else (e.g., not-so-normal insects).

Step 4: Evaluate the Answer Choices

(E) validates the author's assumption. By getting trapped in awkward positions, insects in real amber are more likely to look bizarre, bolstering the author's claim that normal-looking insects are more likely the sign of a fake.

(A) suggests that there's a good chance that forgeries will get sold, but does nothing to support the idea that normal-looking insects are any indication of a fake.

(B) is an Irrelevant Comparison. Here, size doesn't matter. The argument is all about spotting fakes.

(C) is an Irrelevant Comparison. Whether insects are worth more than plants or not, the argument is about recognizing fakes. This adds nothing to that argument.

(D) is a 180. The author is suggesting otherwise, saying you can spot a fake merely by looking at how normal the insect inside the amber appears.

8. (A) Principle (Identify/Strengthen)

Step 1: Identify the Question Type

The question directly asks for a principle, and one that will "justify" the given argument. That makes this a common Identify the Principle question that acts like a Strengthen question. The correct answer will be a broader take on the specific argument provided.

Step 2: Untangle the Stimulus

The author is concerned about the surge in crimes due to the Internet. The Internet is impersonal, so people are liable to loosen their morals and decide it's okay to hurt other people. Because of this, the author concludes that people should be educated about proper Internet ethics.

Step 3: Make a Prediction

Specifically, the author is advocating for education about the Internet to curb people's immorality. As a general rule (i.e., a principle), the author assumes that education can somehow affect people's morals.

Step 4: Evaluate the Answer Choices

(A) works. If education increases one's sense of moral responsibility, then that would justify the author's proposal to solve the moral problems caused by the Internet.

(B) is Out of Scope. The author's solution is about educating people. Creating a set of guidelines is not the same thing.

(C) is a 180. If educating people *increased* the amount of harm they could cause, that would make matters worse.

(D) is irrelevant. What acts people are morally opposed to have no bearing on whether education will help restore morality.

(E) is Out of Scope. The argument is not concerned with placing blame. It's about taking action to prevent moral lapses.

9. (B) Assumption (Sufficient)

Step 1: Identify the Question Type

According to the question, the argument given is proper "if" the correct answer "is assumed." That makes this a Sufficient Assumption question. Look for an answer that logically connects the evidence to the conclusion.

Step 2: Untangle the Stimulus

The columnist starts right off with the conclusion: video games are not art. The evidence is that video games are interactive, and art requires an experience controlled by the artist.

Step 3: Make a Prediction

Art requires an experience controlled by the artist. If video games did not have that necessary control, then the author can justly conclude that they're not art. However, the author merely states that video games are interactive. So, the author assumes that interactivity somehow takes away the artist's control, which would then solidify the conclusion that video games are not art.

Step 4: Evaluate the Answer Choices

(B) is the author's assumption, suggesting that a video game's interactivity prevents its artist from having the control needed to make it art.

(A) is Out of Scope. Nothing in the argument addresses the creators' intentions.

(C) is a 180. The author implies that video games *can* produce a rich aesthetic experience, and this would allow video games to be art, contrary to the author's point.

(D) is irrelevant. Art is not said to be dependent on *who* creates it, but whether that person has *control*.

(E) is a 180 at worst. If the players' choices are irrelevant, that makes it more likely that the experience *is* ultimately controlled by the creator, thus contradicting the author's point.

10. (C) Strengthen/Weaken (Evaluate the Argument)

Step 1: Identify the Question Type

This question asks for something that will "help in evaluating" the given argument. This is a variation on Strengthen/Weaken questions called Evaluate the Argument. The correct answer will be something that questions the assumption. The answer to that question will determine whether the argument is strong or weak.

Step 2: Untangle the Stimulus

Rumors are swirling that, after detergents with phosphates were banned in a local town, some rebels went to another town to buy their precious phosphate-filled detergents. However, the author has a theory: some people *did* follow the law and went phosphate-free. The evidence is that there was less phosphate in the wastewater.

Step 3: Make a Prediction

Does the reduction in phosphate levels really indicate a switch to phosphate-free detergents, or is the author overlooking another reason why the phosphate levels dipped? The author assumes it's all about the switch, and the correct answer will question if this is the case.

Step 4: Evaluate the Answer Choices

(C) raises a perfect question. What if the wastewater treatment plant treated phosphates differently? If it did, perhaps its new policies are responsible for the lower phosphate levels, hurting the author's claim that it was about people switching detergents. However, if the plant made no changes, then maybe people *did* switch, and the author's claim is supported.

(A) offers no help. The motive for those who defied the new regulation does nothing to determine if other people were following the rules or not.

(B) is Out of Scope. The argument is entirely dependent on phosphate levels. Other pollutants add no value.

(D) doesn't help. It doesn't matter whether wastewater makes up a majority or a small portion of phosphate pollution overall. The argument is about what led to the drop in phosphates in that wastewater.

(E) doesn't help. Whether officials tried to step in or not, the question remains: were there people who switched detergents?

11. (B) Main Point

Step 1: Identify the Question Type

The question asks for the "conclusion of the argument," making this a Main Point question.

Step 2: Untangle the Stimulus

Genetically engineered plants are risky because, at any moment, concerns can be raised that would destroy people's trust in those foods. Prices for such foods aren't high enough to offset the risk, making such crops a bad idea for farmers.

Step 3: Make a Prediction

Note the complete lack of Conclusion Keywords. Each sentence leads to the next with no transition. In a case like this, the One-Sentence Test is needed. What is the one sentence supported by everything else? That's often the most opinionated claim, and that would be the second sentence here: it is unwise for farmers to grow such crops. Why is it unwise? *Because* such crops bring along a great amount of risk (sentence 1), and *because* their prices are not high enough to make up for that risk (sentence 3). Adding *because* before those claims confirms that they work more as evidence in support of the main point: farmers should not grow genetically engineered plants.

Step 4: Evaluate the Answer Choices

(B) perfectly paraphrases the conclusion.

(A) is evidence, not the conclusion. The risk is evidence *why* it's an unwise idea. Some may note that this claim is supported by its own piece of evidence ("because at any time ..."). So, this is *a* conclusion, but it is merely a subsidiary conclusion that in turn supports the main conclusion.

(C) is evidence, not the conclusion. The lack of compensation is *why* growing such crops is unwise.

(D) is preceded by the word *because* in the stimulus, indicating that it's evidence.

(E) is a Distortion. The author states that studies *could* be published that would diminish consumer confidence, but there's no claim that this is already the case.

12. (B) Principle (Parallel)

Step 1: Identify the Question Type

The word *principle* indicates a Principle question. However, the passage "illustrates" a principle that the correct answer will also illustrate. That makes this a Parallel Principle question. Start by expressing the stimulus in broad terms, and look for an answer that applies that same broad idea to a new topic.

Step 2: Untangle the Stimulus

Vaccination involves exposing patients to a mild pathogen so that they develop a resistance to that pathogen and avoid a harsher reaction in the future.

Step 3: Make a Prediction

Start by taking out the "pathogen" context to come up with a broader idea: in order to reduce the effect of a problem in the future, people are exposed to a minor form early on to build up their resistance to the problem. The correct answer will follow this principle, but in a new context.

Step 4: Evaluate the Answer Choices

(B) matches the principle perfectly. To reduce the effect of a problem in the future (treachery and cruelty), people are exposed to a minor form early on (as allegories in fairy tales) to build up their resistance to the problem (make them less vulnerable).

(A) doesn't match. In this case, instead of exposing people to a mild form of something, directors are taking something away.

(C) is a 180. Instead of using a milder form of something to address a problem, the firefighters are creating something *more* intense.

(D) doesn't match. Instead of exposing people to a milder form of something, the business is taking something away.

(E) is a Distortion. In this case, police are using a minor form of a problem to encourage people to avoid more serious forms. This is not the same as helping people become better able to handle the problem.

13. (B) Inference

Step 1: Identify the Question Type

The correct answer fills in the blank in the stimulus, which is preceded by the phrase "it follows that." That means what fills the blank will be directly backed up by the information before it, which makes it an Inference.

Step 2: Untangle the Stimulus

When nations don't interact much, they don't really understand each other's needs and problems, and sympathy and justice depend on that understanding.

Step 3: Make a Prediction

A lack of interaction impedes understanding, which is necessary for sympathy and justice. If understanding is that important, then losing it would have a major effect on sympathy and justice. So, what follows (and should therefore fill in the blank) is that those countries that barely interact are short on the needed understanding, which is going to affect their ability to share sympathy and justice.

Step 4: Evaluate the Answer Choices

(B) adequately expresses the potential consequence of little to no interaction.

(A) distorts the Formal Logic. Sympathy and justice *depend on* understanding, which means understanding is necessary. But that doesn't make such understanding enough to guarantee that there *will* be sympathy and justice.

(C) is Extreme. Nations that don't interact may not share sympathy or justice, but there's nothing to suggest that this is the root of "almost all" of their problems.

(D) is an Extreme Distortion. The stimulus mentions nothing about eliminating conflict and never suggests that there's *no way* to do so.

(E) is Extreme. This suggests that nations *must* have interaction to know a little about each other. However, while the stimulus does mention how little knowledge countries have with little interaction, it's still possible for nations to have some trace of understanding even with no interaction at all.

14. (A) Flaw

Step 1: Identify the Question Type

The question directly asks for a flaw in the activist's argument.

Step 2: Untangle the Stimulus

The activist is concerned about pollutants in the water that contribute to incurable cancer and birth defects. The activist wants to "significantly" reduce these problems and concludes "Clearly" that shutting down polluting industries is the only solution. The evidence is that these industries wouldn't comply with regulations.

Step 3: Make a Prediction

Saying that this is the *only* solution is a sure sign that the activist is overlooking something. While there *is* a link between pollutants and health problems, pollutants may not be the *only* factor—and may not even be the most significant factor. The correct answer will address this overlooked possibility.

Step 4: Evaluate the Answer Choices

(A) addresses the issue. If there are other factors that contribute to a significant number of health problems, then the activist loses the ability to claim shutting down factories is the *only* solution.

(B) is Out of Scope. The argument is only about significantly reducing cancer and birth defects in people. The effect of pollutants on other animals is not an issue here.

(C) is a 180. If the activist assumed that there were several different causes, then shutting down industries wouldn't be the *only* solution.

(D) is a Distortion. If industries wouldn't comply with regulations, the activist wouldn't have much reason to believe they would volunteer on their own. And even if they did, this still doesn't address the problem that pollutants might not be the most significant factor in cancer and birth defects.

(E) is Out of Scope. Even if some pollutants *did* have some benefits, there's no indication that they would be beneficial enough to affect the activist's cause of preventing cancer and birth defects.

15. (C) Assumption (Sufficient)

Step 1: Identify the Question Type

The correct answer will complete the argument "if" it is "assumed," making this a Sufficient Assumption question.

Step 2: Untangle the Stimulus

The political leader is convinced that offering a compromise to her opponents will benefit her side. As evidence, the leader presents the two possible outcomes: 1) The opposition agrees, and a compromise is reached. 2) The opposition says no, and they get blamed for failing to compromise.

Step 3: Make a Prediction

The problem is that the leader only directly says that the second outcome (opposition says no) will actually benefit her side. The leader never says that the first outcome (an actual compromise) would be a benefit. The leader assumes as much because, if it *is* a benefit, then her side *does* benefit either way, validating her conclusion.

Step 4: Evaluate the Answer Choices

(C) directly matches the assumption.

(A) is not good enough. A desire to compromise does not necessarily mean a compromise would be beneficial.

(B) is just not enough. If the opposition *never* compromises, then the leader's side is guaranteed a rejection, which would be an automatic benefit. However, "rarely" compromising allows for a possible exception. In that case, there's no guarantee that the compromise would be a benefit.

(D) is Out of Scope. Any benefit to the opposition has no bearing on benefits to the leader's side.

(E) is not enough. Even if the opposition *does* compromise, there's still no evidence that a compromise will certainly benefit the leader's side.

16. (B) Principle (Identify/Strengthen)

Step 1: Identify the Question Type

The question asks for a principle that will "justify" the given argument. That makes this a common Identify the Principle question in which the principle will effectively Strengthen the argument.

Step 2: Untangle the Stimulus

Some people think it's okay to push a remedy even if doesn't work. However, the author argues otherwise, claiming there *is* a danger. Those people using the ineffective remedies could be ignoring solutions that actually help.

Step 3: Make a Prediction

In general terms, something that *seems* harmless can still be harmful if it prevents people from getting something that will actually help.

Step 4: Evaluate the Answer Choices

(B) matches. This makes the ineffective folk remedies harmful because they interfere with something that would benefit people (i.e., effective treatments).

(A) does not match. People do *not* believe that the folk remedies are harmful, so this doesn't apply.

(C) is Out of Scope. The argument is not about blaming people for being dishonest.

(D) is Out of Scope. The author is not placing responsibility on anyone.

(E) is Out of Scope for the same reason as **(D)**. The author is not placing responsibility on anyone.

17. (B) Method of Argument

Step 1: Identify the Question Type

While not a complete question, the phrase "proceeds by" indicates that the question is asking for *how* the argument is made, making this a Method of Argument of question.

Step 2: Untangle the Stimulus

The author takes issue with a radio station that's pushing how popular its new format is. The station cites how much its call-in listeners rave. The author isn't convinced, and compares the station's logic to someone saying a politician is popular based on a survey of that politician's supporters.

Step 3: Make a Prediction

The comparison between the radio station's claim and the politician example is a very common argumentative technique: analogy. The politician situation is clearly absurd: of course a candidate will appear popular if you only talk to people voting for that candidate. The analogy shows how the station's argument is equally absurd: of course the new format will appear popular if you only consider the people

who call your station to make requests. The correct answer will express this use of analogy to highlight flawed reasoning.

Step 4: Evaluate the Answer Choices

(B) accurately described the method. The author refers to a clearly flawed inference (the politician's popularity) to argue against a similar inference (the radio station's claim) via analogy.

(A) is a clever Distortion. The author certainly *implies* that the radio station's results are based on biased feedback. However, the author doesn't directly make that claim. The author hides behind an analogy, and *that* is the way the argument actually proceeds.

(C) is a Distortion. The politician argument does not use the same evidence as the radio station argument, and it's certainly not "more reasonable."

(D) is a 180. The example used is not a *counterexample*. Its logic is consistent with the radio station's and is flawed in the same way to show similarity.

(E) is Out of Scope. The author does not expose any contradiction.

18. (D) Flaw

Step 1: Identify the Question Type

The phrase "vulnerable to criticism" is common LSAT language indicating that something is wrong with the argument. So, this question is asking what that flaw is.

Step 2: Untangle the Stimulus

This historian starts right off with the conclusion: those who deny Shakespeare's authorship are motivated solely by snobbery. As evidence, the historian points out that those naysayers just happen to be descendants of the very upper-class people they claim actually wrote the plays.

Step 3: Make a Prediction

It is rather coincidental that the people making these claims just happen to be descendants. However, the author takes that one step too far by saying their motives are *purely* snobbish. While it is possible that their sense of entitlement is *partially* a factor, there's still a chance they have other motives. The correct answer will address this overlooked possibility.

It's very important to note one thing: while it may seem that the author disagrees with such outrageous claims, the author never outright *states* that these people are wrong. The argument is purely about their motives and not about the actual truth of their claims (making this a variation of the classic ad hominem attack).

Step 4: Evaluate the Answer Choices

(D) is the flaw. The author is too focused on these people's background to consider other, potentially more valid motives.

(A) is an Extreme Distortion. The author never actually addresses the truth of the claims. Even if the author isn't entirely convinced in this case, that's a far cry from assuming that claims motivated by snobbery *cannot* be true.

(B) is not a flaw. If someone *is* "purely motivated" by one thing, then it's perfectly logical to assume that no other motivation exists. The author's actual flaw is saying that these people are purely motivated by snobbery in the first place.

(C) is Out of Scope. The author's argument is solely about the people trying to discredit Shakespeare. The motives of those who *do* give Shakespeare credit are irrelevant.

(E) suggests circular reasoning. However, the author's evidence and assumption are distinct enough from the conclusion. The author's assumption does not require the conclusion to be true.

19. (B) Paradox

Step 1: Identify the Question Type

The question asks for something that "helps to explain" a situation, making this a Paradox question. Look for the central mystery (i.e., *why* does something unexpected happen?), and find an answer that provides a solution.

Step 2: Untangle the Stimulus

The stimulus describes two sets of lemurs. The first live in rain forests with year-round foliage. The second live in forests where leaves fall off the trees in winter. For some reason, the second group is much more active during the night than the first group.

Step 3: Make a Prediction

Paradox questions always boil down to a central mystery. In this case, why is the second group so much more active at night than the first group during the winter? The only known difference is that the second group lives where the leaves are gone in winter, while the first group lives where the leaves stay up year-round. Most likely, there's something about the missing foliage that makes the second group more active at night. Don't try to predict *exactly* what that would be (there are too many possibilities), but know the correct answer will probably tie the increased nighttime activity to the missing leaves.

Step 4: Evaluate the Answer Choices

(B) solves the mystery. If both groups have high-flying predators during the day, then the first group is a little safer during the winter with its canopy of leaves. They can get things done during the day and rest a little more at night. The

second group is more exposed with all the leaves gone. They'd be more likely to avoid going out during the day and wait until night to do their business. That would be why they're more active at night than the first group.

(A) is a 180. This gives both groups equal competition during the day, which should result in equal activity at night. Unless there's something significantly different about one group's competition, the mystery goes unsolved.

(C) is a 180. This puts both groups at equal risk during the day, which would suggest equal activity at night. There's still no understanding why their nighttime activities are different.

(D) brings up a difference between the two groups, but there's no direct connection between size and nighttime activity. If anything, one might expect the larger animals would be more active because they need to eat more, but this would be the complete opposite of what actually happens.

(E) doesn't help. Giving the second group a more limited diet doesn't explain why they would be more active at night. Even if the limited diet makes it harder for the second group to find food, the mystery is why the second group *increases* its nighttime activity so much more—not why it spends more time overall.

20. (B) Role of a Statement

Step 1: Identify the Question Type

The question provides a claim from the stimulus and asks for its "role" in the argument. That makes this a Role of a Statement question.

Step 2: Untangle the Stimulus

The critic presents a common view: "literary" fiction is meant to be interpreted, while "genre" fiction is just for fun. However, the critic argues that these labels are meaningless. Nothing should be interpreted because that diminishes the work's emotional impact.

Step 3: Make a Prediction

The claim in question is the very last sentence. However, that's not the conclusion. By adding the word *because* before it, its role becomes clear: *because* evaluating a work takes away the emotional impact, the critic feels there should be no such interpretation, making the distinction between "literary" and "genre" fiction pointless. That identifies the claim in question as evidence, which is ultimately used to support the critic's conclusion about the labels being improper.

Step 4: Evaluate the Answer Choices

(B) correctly identifies the last sentence as evidence for the critic's conclusion.

(A) is mistaken. The conclusion is that separating "literary" and "genre" fiction is a "specious distinction."

(C) is off because the critic's conclusion is that the distinction between "literary" and "genre" fiction is false. The claim in question is not an implication of that conclusion.

(D) is a Distortion. The only distinction mentioned is that between "literary" and "genre" fiction. However, the critic *disputes* rather than considers that distinction. And the claim in question explains why that distinction is wrong.

(E) is Out of Scope. There's no clear objection that the claim in question seems to address.

21. (A) Strengthen

Step 1: Identify the Question Type

The correct answer will "justify" the application provided, making this a Strengthen question. However, this is a relatively common variation in which a principle is given along with a supposed application of that principle. The application is usually incomplete. The correct answer will fill in the missing piece so that it applies properly.

Step 2: Untangle the Stimulus

The principle is that people who neither fault themselves for a behavior nor promise to stop shouldn't criticize that behavior in others. This supposedly applies to Shimada, who has not promised to stop being late to things, and thus shouldn't criticize McFeney for the same behavior.

Step 3: Make a Prediction

By the principle, criticizing others should be avoided by people who don't promise to stop their own behavior *and don't fault themselves for that behavior*. The application leaves out the part about the lack of self-criticism. For the application to be complete, it must include a claim that Shimada does not fault himself for his tardiness.

Step 4: Evaluate the Answer Choices

(A) fills in the missing piece of the puzzle. If Shimada does not criticize his own tardiness, then that (along with his refusal to vow quitting such behavior) would set off the principle, denying him the right to criticize McFeney.

(B) is Out of Scope. The frequency of the behavior in question is not part of the principle.

(C) is Out of Scope. How McFeney acts toward Shimada has no bearing on applying the principle to Shimada.

(D) is a 180. If Shimada *does* criticize himself, then the principle doesn't apply. It only applies to people who *don't* fault themselves.

(E) is Out of Scope. The frequency of the behavior is not addressed in the principle.

22. (A) Flaw

Step 1: Identify the Question Type

The question directly asks for a flaw in the reasoning.

Step 2: Untangle the Stimulus

The author is arguing for access to multiple newspapers because no individual newspaper could fully cover every story, and every important story should be covered fully.

Step 3: Make a Prediction

The author commits a very subtle scope shift. By the evidence, no single newspaper could fully cover *every single story*. However, the author only states that all sides of *important* stories should be covered. Perhaps one newspaper can cover all sides of the *important* stories, while skimping out on some of the less significant stories. In that case, one newspaper *would* be enough. The author overlooks this possibility, and that's the flaw.

Step 4: Evaluate the Answer Choices

(A) addresses the error. Just because a single newspaper can't fully cover *every* story doesn't mean it can't fully cover every *important* story.

(B) is a Distortion. The author isn't arguing that two newspapers will definitely do the job. It's possible that it would take three, four, or even more newspapers to get the kind of coverage the author expects.

(C) is not accurate. The author's conclusion (people should have access to multiple papers) is not just supported by factual evidence, but also by evidence of what newspapers *should* do (they should cover all sides of important stories).

(D) is Extreme. The author's argument does not depend on people having access to *all* newspapers, just "more than one."

(E) is not a *logical* flaw in the argument. Some people might subjectively believe that the argument should address more than just important studies, but that's not a *reasoning* flaw, which the question asks for.

23. (D) Inference

Step 1: Identify the Question Type

The correct answer "follows logically" from what is given, which means it will be an Inference directly backed up by the stimulus.

Step 2: Untangle the Stimulus

The information discusses a company called Moradco. Most of its mines in Velyena have never violated regulations, while every one of its gold mines worldwide *has* violated regulations.

Step 3: Make a Prediction

The last claim provides a little Formal Logic. If one of Moradco's mines is a gold mine, it has violated regulations:

If   *gold mine*   →   *violate*

By contrapositive, any mine that has *not* violated regulations is *not* a gold mine:

If   *~ violate*   →   *~ gold mine*

By that logic, because most of the mines in Velyena have *not* violated regulations, most of the mines in Velyena must *not* be gold mines.

Step 4: Evaluate the Answer Choices

(D) is the right logical deduction.

(A) is not supported. There's no information on the number of mines Moradco operates anywhere.

(B) is not supported. There's no information on how many total mines Moradco operates anywhere.

(C) is a Distortion. *Most* of the mines in Velyena have never violated regulations. But there could still be plenty that *have* (say 50 of the 500 mines in Velyena). Those mines could all be gold mines and could certainly be the majority of Moradco's worldwide gold mines.

(E) is a Distortion. While most of the mines in Velyena are not gold mines, that could be an exceptional area. It's still possible that Moradco has predominantly gold mines throughout the rest of the world.

24. (A) Assumption (Necessary)

Step 1: Identify the Question Type

The question asks for an "assumption" on which the argument "relies," making this a Necessary Assumption question.

Step 2: Untangle the Stimulus

Tariffs are great for the few people who make the product being taxed. Most people, though, oppose tariffs because they hike up costs. *So,* the author concludes that politicians who vote against tariffs are more likely to be reelected.

Step 3: Make a Prediction

The author took quite a leap. The evidence is just that people don't like tariffs. The conclusion suddenly brings up the reelection of politicians, implying that a vote for tariffs can potentially end a politician's career. The only way this is true is if the anti-tariff folks are so passionate that they insist on voting against politicians who favor tariffs.

Step 4: Evaluate the Answer Choices

(A) must be true, suggesting that opponents are as likely or more likely to base their voting decision on the tariff than anyone else. Using the Denial Test, if this *wasn't* true, opponents would be *less* likely to base their decision on tariffs. In that case, tariffs wouldn't be as big a problem as the author insists.

(B) is not necessary. The argument is not about what politicians *actually* do, but what the author recommends they *should* do.

(C) is Out of Scope. The argument is only discussing product-specific tariffs, not general tariffs.

(D) is Extreme. The author's argument is only about tariffs. There's no need to shun *all* measures that benefit few people.

(E) is not necessary. Whether people know the trouble of tariffs or not has no bearing on the potential reelection of politicians.

25. (D) Inference (EXCEPT)

Step 1: Identify the Question Type

The correct answer will be based on the information given, making this an Inference question. However, unlike most Inference questions that look for something absolutely supported, this one states that four answers *could* be true. The correct answer will be the exception: the one that *cannot* be true based on what's given.

Step 2: Untangle the Stimulus

The author provides a direct relationship between seals and dolphins: the longer one can stay underwater, the deeper one can dive. Then two pairs of animals are compared. Dolphins can dive deeper than fur seals, and elephant seals can stay underwater longer than Weddell seals.

Step 3: Make a Prediction

Start by using the relationship described, then make deductions about the four animals provided. Because dolphins can dive deeper than fur seals, dolphins must be able to stay underwater longer:

dolphins   >   *fur seals*

And because elephants seals can stay underwater longer than Weddell seals, elephant seals can dive deeper:

elephant seals   >   *Weddell seals*

There is *no* connection between the two pairs. For instance, there's no way of knowing whether dolphins can surpass elephant seals and Weddell seals, are inferior to both, or are somewhere in between. The correct answer will lead to an impossible scenario (i.e., one in which fur seals dominate dolphins or Weddell seals dominate elephant seals).

Step 4: Evaluate the Answer Choices

(D) is impossible, and thus the correct answer. If fur seals can surpass elephant seals, then they must also surpass Weddell seals (fur > elephant > Weddell). However, dolphins surpass fur seals, which means they would be able to stay submerged the longest and dive the deepest of all (dolphins > fur > elephant > Weddell). In this scenario, there's no way Weddell seals could surpass dolphins.

(A) is possible. This would rank dolphins in between elephant seals and Weddell seals (elephant > dolphin > Weddell). Then, fur seals would just have to be inferior to dolphins, too. That's fine.

(B) is possible. This would rank Weddell seals between dolphins and fur seals (dolphin > Weddell > fur). Then, elephant seals would just have to be superior to Weddell seals, too. That's fine.

(C) is possible. This would rank Weddell seals superior to dolphins and fur seals (Weddell > dolphin; Weddell > fur). Then, elephant seals would just have to be superior to Weddell seals. That's fine.

(E) is possible. This would rank fur seals between elephant seals and Weddell seals (elephant > fur > Weddell). Then, fur seals would just have to be inferior to dolphins, too. That's fine.

Section III: Logic Games

Game 1: Community Festival Performances

Q#	Question Type	Correct	Difficulty
1	Acceptability	A	★
2	"If" / Could Be True	B	★
3	Must Be False (CANNOT Be True)	D	★★
4	Earliest	C	★
5	Complete and Accurate List	C	★

Game 2: Ceramic Bowl Display

Q#	Question Type	Correct	Difficulty
6	Acceptability	E	★
7	"If" / Could Be True	D	★
8	"If" / Must Be True	C	★
9	"If" / Must Be True	A	★
10	"If" / Must Be False (CANNOT Be True)	B	★★
11	Must Be True	B	★★★
12	"If" / Must Be True	A	★

Game 3: Office Selection

Q#	Question Type	Correct	Difficulty
13	Partial Acceptability	B	★★★
14	Must Be True	C	★★★
15	Could Be True	A	★★★★
16	"If" / Could Be True	E	★★★
17	Must Be True	E	★★★

Game 4: Community Committee Volunteers

Q#	Question Type	Correct	Difficulty
18	Partial Acceptability	E	★
19	"If" / Could Be True EXCEPT	C	★★
20	Must Be True EXCEPT	B	★★★
21	"If" / Complete and Accurate List	B	★★★
22	Completely Determine	C	★★★
23	Rule Substitution	C	★★★

Game 1: Community Festival Performances

Step 1: Overview

Situation: Entertainers performing at a community festival

Entities: Six entertainers (Robinson, Shahpari, Tigay, Wu, Yeaton, Zane)

Action: Strict Sequencing. Determine the order in which the entertainers perform.

Limitations: No two entertainers perform at the same time, so this is one-to-one Sequencing. However, the schedule is split in that the first three performances are in the morning and the last three are in the afternoon.

Step 2: Sketch

List the entities by initial and set up six numbered slots in order, using the times provided. Draw a line to separate the morning and afternoon slots, labeling each side.

```
         R S T W Y Z
     morn    |    aft
    ___ ___ ___ | ___ ___ ___
     9  10  11  |  2   3   4
```

Alternatively, you could list the morning slots above the afternoon slots to indicate morning and afternoon. Choose whichever configuration is your preference.

```
            R S T W Y Z
    morn   ___ ___ ___
            9  10  11
    aft    ___ ___ ___
            2   3   4
```

Step 3: Rules

Rule 1 sets up a loose relationship: Robinson performs sometime before Zane.

```
        R . . . Z
```

That means Robinson cannot perform last (4:00 P.M.), and Zane cannot perform first (9:00 A.M.). If helpful, add "~ R" and "~ Z" under the respective slots.

Rule 2 creates a block: Yeaton must perform immediately after Wu:

```
        [WY]
```

That means Wu cannot perform last (4:00 P.M.), and Yeaton cannot perform first (9:00 A.M.). Again, if helpful, add "~ W" and "~ Y" under the respective slots.

Rule 3 limits Tigay to the afternoon. Draw "~ T" under the first three slots, or draw T above the last three slots with arrows pointing to the slots.

Rule 4 limits Zane to the morning. Draw "~ Z" under the last three slots, or draw Z above the first three slots with arrows pointing to the slots.

Step 4: Deductions

The Duplication of Zane in Rules 1 and 4 is significant. If Zane is restricted to the morning and Robinson has to perform before Zane, then Robinson is also restricted to the morning. That means Robinson and Zane will be two of the three morning performers. The third morning performer cannot be Tigay (Rule 3). That leaves Shahpari, Wu, and Yeaton. Shahpari is a Floater—which you can mark with a star or other notation in the list of entities—and could certainly be the third morning performer. Wu could be also, as long as Yeaton performs immediately afterward in the afternoon (Rule 2). Yeaton could not perform in the morning because there would not also be space for Wu immediately before Yeaton given that Robinson and Zane are already in the morning, so Yeaton cannot be the third morning performer. Thus, Yeaton must perform in the afternoon.

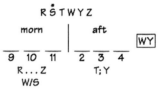

It's possible to set up Limited Options depending on who performs with Robinson and Zane in the morning (Wu or Shahpari). However, as long as the previously mentioned deductions are made, Limited Options are nice but ultimately not needed.

Step 5: Questions

1. (A) Acceptability

As with any Acceptability question, use the rules one at a time to eliminate answers that violate those rules.

(E) violates Rule 1 by having Robinson scheduled after Zane. **(D)** violates Rule 2 by scheduling Tigay in between Wu and Yeaton. **(C)** violates Rule 3 by scheduling Tigay third, which would be in the morning. **(B)** violates Rule 4 by scheduling Zane fourth, which would be in the afternoon. That leaves **(A)** as the correct answer.

2. (B) "If" / Could Be True

For this question, Wu must perform in the morning. By Rule 4, so must Zane, which means so must Robinson (Rule 1). That fills up the morning, leaving Shahpari, Tigay, and Yeaton for the afternoon. By Rule 2, Yeaton must perform *immediately* after Wu. The only way to do that is to have Wu perform at 11:00 A.M. and Yeaton at 2:00 P.M. That leaves Robinson and Zane to perform at 9:00 A.M. and 10:00 A.M., respectively. Shahpari and Tigay will perform at 3:00 P.M. and 4:00 P.M., in either order.

$$\frac{R}{9} \quad \frac{Z}{10} \quad \frac{W}{11} \quad \Big| \quad \frac{Y}{2} \quad \frac{S/T}{3} \quad \frac{T/S}{4}$$

In that case, only **(B)** is possible, making it the correct answer. The other answers all must be false.

3. (D) Must Be False (CANNOT Be True)
The correct answer will be a time at which Shahpari is unable to perform. The remaining answers will list times at which Shahpari *could* perform.

By the work in the second question, Shahpari could perform at 3:00 P.M. That eliminates **(E)**. If Shahpari performed in the morning, it could be at any time, with Robinson and Zane performing at the remaining two morning times. That eliminates **(A)**, **(B)**, and **(C)**, leaving **(D)** as the correct answer. For further proof:

If Shahpari performs in the afternoon, the only person left to perform in the morning with Robinson and Zane would be Wu. In that case (as seen in the second question), Wu would have to perform at 11:00 A.M. so that Yeaton could perform immediately afterward (Rule 2) at 2:00 P.M. That would force Shahpari elsewhere, unable to perform at 2:00 P.M.

4. (C) Earliest
The correct answer to this question will be the earliest time at which Wu could perform. As seen in the second question, Wu could perform as early as 11:00 A.M., which eliminates **(D)** and **(E)**. In fact, that's the earliest Wu could perform. If Wu performed earlier in the morning, then Yeaton would also perform in the morning (Rule 2), along with Zane (Rule 4) and thus Robinson (Rule 1). That would be too many performers in the morning. Therefore, the only time (and thus the earliest time) Wu could perform in the morning is 11:00 A.M., making **(C)** the correct answer.

5. (C) Complete and Accurate List
The correct answer to this question will list every entertainer that must perform in the afternoon. By Rule 3, that list must include Tigay. The list must also include Yeaton. After all, if Yeaton performed in the morning, so would Wu (Rule 2), as would Zane (Rule 4) and thus Robinson (Rule 1). That would be too many morning performers.

The correct answer to the Acceptability question has Shahpari perform in the morning, and the second question has Wu perform in the morning. Thus, neither Shahpari nor Wu has to perform in the afternoon. Furthermore, Robinson and Zane can never perform in the afternoon. That means Tigay and Yeaton are the only people who must perform in the afternoon, making **(C)** the correct answer.

Game 2: Ceramic Bowl Display

Step 1: Overview

Situation: A selection of crafted ceramic bowls being put on display

Entities: Eight potters (Larsen, Mills, Neiman, Olivera, Park, Reigel, Serra, Vance)

Action: Sequencing/Selection Hybrid. Determine which of the bowls will be displayed (Selection), and place the selected bowls in order (Sequencing).

Limitations: There are eight bowls, each one crafted by one of the eight potters. For the Selection element, exactly six of the eight bowls will be chosen. For the Sequencing element, there are six consecutively numbered positions, one bowl per position.

Step 2: Sketch

For the Sequencing element, a set of six numbered slots will suffice. For the Selection element, simply list the potters by initial and note that six out of the eight will be selected. As the game proceeds, circle potters whose bowls are chosen and cross out those whose bowls are not chosen.

```
        L M N O P R S V    -Pick 6

        ___ ___ ___ ___ ___ ___
         1   2   3   4   5   6
```

Step 3: Rules

Rule 1 affects the selection. If Larsen's bowl is selected, then Mills's bowl cannot be. By contrapositive, if Mills's bowl is selected, then Larsen's bowl cannot be. Essentially, that means the display cannot include both Larsen's and Mills's bowls.

```
        L → ~M
        M → ~L    (Never LM)
```

Note that this does not mean the display must include one of their bowls. Only six bowls are selected, so it's possible that both of their bowls are rejected.

Rule 2 places a major restriction on Park's bowl. If it's included in the display, it has to be next to both Olivera's and Serra's bowl (i.e., in between those two bowls). The order of Olivera's and Serra's bowls are not defined.

```
        P → OPS or SPO
```

This means that Park's bowl cannot be placed on either end, so add "~ P" under slots 1 and 6.

Rule 3 restricts Reigel's bowl to position 1 or 6. This does *not* mean that Reigel's bowl is definitely selected. So, it's still possible for two other bowls to be placed in positions 1 and 6, with Reigel's bowl not selected. However, it can be noted that Reigel's bowl will not be placed in positions 2–5. Draw "~ R" under those slots and/or make a shorthand rule to the side.

```
        R → 1 or 6
```

Rule 4 prevents Serra's bowl from being placed in position 2 or 4. Again, Serra's bowl is not definitely selected. However, if it is, it cannot be placed in position 2 or 4. Add "~ S" under those two slots.

Rule 5 restricts Neiman's bowl to one position: fifth. It's still possible that Neiman's bowl won't be selected. However, if it is, it must go in position 5.

```
        N → 5
```

Step 4: Deductions

There are a couple of opportunities for Limited Options in this game, most notably based on the last rule. If Neiman's bowl is selected, that establishes a bowl in position 5, which does place a significant restriction on Park's bowl, but leads to no further concrete deductions. If Neiman's bowl is *not* selected, that helps limit whose bowl *is* selected, but allows for no absolute placement.

While Limited Options are always worth considering, a glance ahead reveals that, of the game's seven questions, five are "If" questions and one is an Acceptability question. Those questions will provide a lot of information, so it's more important now to pay attention to significant entities and any Numbers restrictions.

The only entity Duplicated in the rules is Serra. By Rule 2, if Park's bowl was selected, Serra's bowl would have to be next to it. However, Serra's bowl cannot be in position 2 or 4 (Rule 4), which means Park's bowl cannot be in position 3. Also by Rule 2, Park's bowl cannot be on the end because it needs to be in between two other bowls. That limits Park's bowl to positions 2, 4, and 5. However, Park's bowl can also go unselected, leaving too many options to consider.

In terms of Numbers, six bowls must be selected, but the selection cannot include both Larsen's and Mills's (so you could almost treat them as one entity labeled as "L/M" in the entities list). That means at least one of their bowls will go unselected. That leaves only one more bowl that can go unselected. Once that second bowl is determined, then everyone else's bowl must be selected. This will be a significant point throughout the game. Finally, the only entity that has no rules about it is Vance's bowl, so you can mark it with a star in the list of entities to indicate that it is a Floater.

If you opted to include all the negative deductions, a final Master Sketch would look something like this:

```
        L/M N O P R S V     -Pick 6
                              P → OPS or SPO
        ___ ___ ___ ___ ___ ___
         1   2   3   4   5   6
        ~P  ~R  ~R  ~R  ~R  ~P
            ~S  ~P  ~S  [N]
```

Step 5: Questions

6. (E) Acceptability

As with any Acceptability question, go through the rules one at a time, eliminating answers that violate those rules.

(A) violates Rule 1 by including Larsen's bowl but also including Mills's bowl. **(D)** violates Rule 2 by not placing Park's bowl next to Olivera's bowl. **(C)** violates Rule 3 by putting Reigel's bowl in position 5—it is supposed to be limited to position 1 or 6. No remaining answers violate Rule 4, but **(B)** violates Rule 5 by putting Neiman's bowl in position 2—it is supposed to be limited to position 5. That leaves **(E)** as the correct answer.

7. (D) "If" / Could Be True

For this question, Neiman's bowl and Park's bowl are selected. By Rule 5, Neiman's bowl must go in position 5. Park's bowl has to be surrounded by Olivera's and Serra's (Rule 2), which means Park's bowl cannot go in position 1 or 6. Park's bowl cannot go into position 4 because Neiman's bowl is in the way. Park's bowl cannot go in position 3, because Serra's bowl couldn't be in either position next to it (Rule 4). Therefore, Park's bowl would have to be in position 2, placing Olivera's and Serra's bowls in positions 1 and 3, in either order.

L /M (N)O (P)R (S)V

O/S	P	S/O		N	
1	2	3	4	5	6

With that, the only bowls that could be in position 1 are Olivera's or Serra's, making **(D)** the correct answer.

8. (C) "If" / Must Be True

For this question, Larsen's bowl is established in position 6, and Olivera's bowl is established in position 2. With Larsen's bowl included, Mills's bowl must be out (Rule 1)—cross it off the entity list for this new sketch. Placing Olivera's bowl in position 2 limits the placement of Park's bowl. By Rule 2, Park's bowl would have to be next to Olivera's bowl in position 1 or 3. However, Park's bowl would also have to be next to Serra's bowl, which means it cannot be in position 1. In addition, putting Park's bowl in position 3 would put Serra's bowl in position 4, which violates Rule 4. Therefore, Park's bowl cannot be included—cross it off the entity list, too. With Mills's and Park's bowls eliminated, everyone else's bowl must be selected. That includes Neiman, Reigel, Serra, and Vance. Neiman's bowl would have to be in position 5 (Rule 5). With Larsen's bowl in position 6, Reigel's bowl would have to be in position 1 (Rule 3). Serra's bowl can't be in position 4 (Rule 4), so Vance's bowl must go there, placing Serra's bowl in position 3.

(L)/M(N)(O)X(R)(S)(V)

R	O	S	V	N	L
1	2	3	4	5	6

With Serra's bowl established in position 3, **(C)** is the correct answer.

9. (A) "If" / Must Be True

For this question, Park's bowl is in position 4. By Rule 2, that means Olivera's and Serra's bowls must be in positions 3 and 5, in either order. With position 5 filled, there's no place left for Neiman's bowl. So, Neiman's bowl must be eliminated—cross it off the entity list for this new sketch. That leaves the bowls of Larsen, Mills, Reigel, and Vance. Given that only one of Larsen's and Mills's bowls can be chosen, the bowls of Reigel and Vance both must be chosen.

L /M X(O)(P)R(S)V

		O/S	P	S/O	
1	2	3	4	5	6
	~R				

Reigel's bowl cannot be displayed in position 2 (Rule 3). So, the only bowls left that can fill position 2 are Larsen's, Mills's, and Vance's, making **(A)** the correct answer.

10. (B) "If" / Must Be False (CANNOT Be True)

For this question, Larsen's bowl will be in position 1 and Olivera's bowl will be in position 4. With Larsen's bowl included, Mills's bowl must be out (Rule 1). Only one more bowl needs to be eliminated.

(L)X/M(N)(O)P R (S) V

L			O		
1	2	3	4	5	6

Olivera's bowl limits the placement of Park's bowl, which would have to be surrounded by both Olivera's and Serra's bowls if included (Rule 2). So, Park's bowl could only be in position 3 or 5. However, if Park's bowl was in position 3, Serra's bowl would have to be in position 2, violating Rule 4. If Park's bowl were in position 5, Serra's bowl would be in position 6. However, that would leave no place for Neiman's bowl (Rule 5) or Reigel's bowl (Rule 3). That would eliminate too many bowls. There is no position to place Park's bowl. Therefore, Park's bowl must be the second bowl eliminated, making **(B)** the correct answer.

11. (B) Must Be True

The correct answer will be a potter whose bowl *must* be selected. The remaining four answers will list potters whose bowls could be left out.

Previous work helps make short work of this question. The correct answer to the Acceptability question and the sketch for the fourth question of the set show that Neiman's bowl need not be selected. That eliminates **(A)**. For the fifth question of the set, Park's bowl was left out. That eliminates **(C)**.

A little extra work with the sketch from the second question of the set puts an end to the testing. In that case, if either

Larsen's or Mills's bowl is in position 4, then either Reigel's or Vance's bowl could be in position 6.

O/S	P	S/O	L/M	N	R/V
1	2	3	4	5	6

In that case, either Reigel's bowl or Vance's bowl could be left out, eliminating **(D)** and **(E)**. That leaves **(B)** as the correct answer. For further proof that Olivera must be there:

If Olivera's bowl was left out, then Park's bowl couldn't be displayed (Rule 2). That would mean everyone else's bowl would have to be included: Larsen's, Mills's, Neiman's, Reigel's, Serra's, and Vance's. However, that would violate Rule 1 by including Larsen's bowl with Mills's. That's unacceptable, so Olivera's bowl cannot be left out, which means it must be included.

12. (A) "If" / Must Be True

For this question, the display will include Neiman's, Park's, and Reigel's bowls. The sketch from the second question of the set already set up what would happen if Neiman's and Park's bowls were included. Neiman's bowl would be in position 5, and Park's bowl would have to be in position 2, with Olivera's and Serra's bowls in positions 1 and 3, in either order.

This question merely adds Reigel's bowl to that display. With position 1 filled, that leaves only position 6 for Reigel's bowl (Rule 3).

L /M Ⓝ Ⓞ Ⓟ Ⓡ Ⓢ V

O/S	P	S/O		N	R
1	2	3	4	5	6

With that, Reigel's bowl is definitely next to Neiman's bowl, making **(A)** the correct answer. **(B)**, **(D)**, and **(E)** all could be true with Vance's bowl in position 5, and **(C)** must be false.

Game 3: Office Selection

Step 1: Overview

Situation: Employees putting in requests for a new office

Entities: Four employees (Jackson, Larabee, Paulson, Torillo) and four offices (W, X, Y, Z)

Action: Sequencing/Matching Hybrid. Determine the order in which the employees select offices (Sequencing), and which office each employee selects (Matching). The employee rankings add a challenging wrinkle to this game, but they are nothing more than a series of limitations used to determine the assignment of offices. Ultimately, there's no action beyond the classic order-and-assign setup. Some may feel the employee rankings add a Process element to the game. However, Process games generally involve a repeated action, which this game does not have. Additionally, because each office is used exactly once, some may feel it is a Sequencing/Distribution Hybrid instead. However, a typical Sequencing/Distribution game has a sequence within each group—not a single sequence of entities with a second type of entity assigned to the first type. In the end, it's more important to understand what needs to be accomplished than to insist on applying an absolute label to the game.

Limitations: The overview provides no clear limitations. All restrictions in this game are clarified in the rules.

Step 2: Sketch

The ultimate goal is to determine the order in which the employees select offices and determine which office each employee selects. To display that, set up two rows. The employees will be entered on top, with their office selections entered below. (Two rows of slots would also work.)

```
          1   2   3   4
   JLPT  ___ ___ ___ ___
   wxyz
```

Step 3: Rules

Rule 1 prevents two people from selecting the same office. So, each office will be selected just once.

Rule 2 limits each employee to just one office. So, no employee can get greedy and choose two offices.

Rule 3 is the most significant. When it's an employee's turn to select an office, that employee will choose the first available office listed in his or her personal ranking.

Step 4: Deductions

The key to this game is understanding how Rule 3 works and affects the selection. The first person selected will get first choice of office. That person will choose the office he or she has ranked highest.

The second employee gets to choose from whatever offices remain. If that employee's top choice is available, the employee will select that office. Otherwise, that employee will settle for the office he or she ranked second. Either way, the second employee will get one of the top two offices on his or her list.

The third employee may still be able to get his or her first choice, if it's still available. If not, the third employee may be able to choose the second office on his or her list. If *that's* not available, the third employee will have to settle for the third office on his or her list.

The final employee is stuck with whatever office is left at the end—regardless of where that employee ranked it.

1	2	3	4
1st rank	1st or 2nd rank	1st or 2nd or 3rd rank	Any rank

So, as an example, if Jackson goes first, Jackson would choose Y—the top-ranked choice on Jackson's list. If Larabee goes second, Larabee would then choose X because it's still available and it's the highest ranked office on Larabee's list. However, if Jackson chooses Y and Paulson goes second, Paulson cannot also choose Y (Rule 1). So, Paulson would have to choose the *next* office on Paulson's list: Z. This goes on until all offices are assigned.

With four employees and no restriction to their order, there are 24 possible outcomes. It's not worth considering all 24 ahead of time, but it is interesting to note two things:

Each employee has ranked office X or Y highest. So, whoever goes first will certainly choose one of those offices. Additionally, nobody ranks W first or second, so W will never be chosen first or second. Furthermore, the only person who ranks W third is Larabee—and even if Larabee goes third, there's no way for X and Z to both be unavailable. So, as it turns out, W will always be the last office selected—which also means that the final office will always be someone's third or fourth choice.

```
          1    2   3   4
   JLPT  ___  ___ ___ ___
   wxyz  x/y          w
```

Step 5: Questions

13. (B) Partial Acceptability

The correct answer will list an acceptable selection of offices by the employees. The remaining answers will all be impossible. This would appear to be a standard Acceptability question, but the answers leave out one critical piece of information: the order in which the selection occurs.

Order or not, none of the answers violate the first two rules. Each answer lists one office per person, and no office is duplicated. That means all answers have to violate Rule 3. The only way to test that is to compare answers to the rankings provided in the overview and try to determine the order in which the selections were made.

For starters, whoever went first would have chosen his or her highest ranked office. That eliminates **(A)** and **(C)**, in which no one did that. In **(B)**, the only person who chose his or her highest ranked office is Larabee, who chose X. So, Larabee must have chosen first. After that, Jackson's and Paulson's highest preference would still be available, but not Torillo's. The next office on Torillo's list is Y, which is what Torillo chose. So, that works. With X and Y chosen, Jackson could go third, forced to choose the highest available office on Jackon's list: Z. That would leave W for Paulson.

	1	2	3	4
JLPT	L	T	J	P
wxyz	x	y	z	w

This answer works fine, making **(B)** the correct answer. For the record:

In **(D)** and **(E)**, the only person who chose his or her highest ranked office is Jackson, who chose Y. So, Jackson chose first in each answer. However, if either Larabee or Torillo went second, that person would get his or her highest preference: X. That doesn't happen in either answer, which means Paulson went second. With Y taken, Paulson would have to settle for the next office on Paulson's list: Z. However, both answers show Paulson choosing X. That can't happen, so both answers are impossible.

14. (C) Must Be True

The correct answer to this question must be true. The remaining answers may be possible, but could also be false.

Whoever goes first will certainly choose the office he or she ranked highest. So, at least that person has to get top choice, making **(C)** the correct answer. For the record:

If Jackson and Larabee go first and second, they could both choose their highest ranked offices (Y and X, respectively). Thus, more than one employee can choose the highest ranked office, which eliminates **(A)**.

In that same scenario, Torillo could go third, having to settle for the office ranked third on Torillo's list: Z. That would leave W for Paulson. Nobody would get the office ranked second on his or her list, which eliminates **(D)**.

	1	2	3	4
JLPT	J	L	T	P
wxyz	y	x	z	w
rank	1st	1st	3rd	4th

If Paulson goes first, Paulson would choose Y. After that, Jackson could go and would have to settle for the second office on Jackson's list: X. Then Larabee could go and would also have to settle for an office ranked second: Z. Thus, more than one employee can choose an office ranked second, which eliminates **(B)**.

In that same scenario, Torillo would have to go fourth, settling for W—the last office on Torillo's list. Nobody would get the office ranked third on his or her list, which eliminates **(E)**.

	1	2	3	4
JLPT	P	J	L	T
wxyz	y	x	z	w
rank	1st	2nd	2nd	4th

15. (A) Could Be True

The correct answer for this question merely *could* be true. The wrong answers will all be impossible.

The first employee gets top choice, while the second employee gets his or her second choice, at worst. Only the last two employees might have to resort to their third choice. This could happen if Jackson goes third and chooses office Z. That would mean the first two employees chose Y and X (e.g., Paulson choosing Y first, then Torillo choosing X). If that happened, Larabee could go last. With X and Z chosen, Larabee would also settle for an office ranked third: W.

	1	2	3	4
JLPT	P	T	J	L
wxyz	y	x	z	w
rank	1st	1st	3rd	3rd

This is possible, making **(A)** the correct answer. For the record:

Only the last employee to choose is in danger of getting the office he or she ranked fourth. That's one employee and no more, which eliminates **(B)** and **(E)**. Similarly, only the last two employees could get stuck with the office they ranked third, and no more than that. That eliminates **(D)**.

There are only three offices ranked second on any employee's list: X, Y, and Z. The only way all of these employees get their second choice is for the first employee to choose the remaining office: W. However, no employee has W as a top option, so this can't happen. That eliminates **(C)**.

16. (E) "If" / Could Be True

For this question, Paulson selects office W. That's the last office on Paulson's list, which means the remaining employees must all select the other offices before Paulson goes. That means Paulson goes last.

	1	2	3	4
JLPT				P
wxyz				w

As usual, whoever goes first will get the office he or she ranked first. The second person will get an office he or she ranked first or second. The third person will get an office he or she ranked first, second, or third. Because of that, only one employee can get the office he or she ranked third, which eliminates **(B)**.

The three people remaining are Jackson, Larabee, and Torillo. If two of those people choose the office they ranked second, the remaining person would be first and get his or her top choice. However, this can't happen. Jackson's and Larabee's second choices would be X and Z, but Torillo would have chosen X first. Jackson's and Torillo's second choices would be X and Y, but Larabee would have chosen X first. And Larabee's and Torillo's second choices would be Y and Z, but Jackson would have chosen Y first. Therefore, **(A)** is impossible.

Three people cannot select their highest ranked office because each employee only has X or Y as a top choice—and only one person can get each office. That eliminates **(C)**.

X is Jackson's second choice, so Jackson couldn't go first and choose X. Neverthless, if Jackson doesn't go first here, then Larabee or Torillo would, and either one of them would choose X first before Jackson gets a chance. So, Jackson won't get office X, which eliminates **(D)**.

That leaves **(E)** as the correct answer, which could happen if Torillo goes first and chooses X, leaving Larabee with the office Larabee ranked second: Z.

	1	2	3	4
JLPT	T	L	J	P
wxyz	x	z	y	w

17. (E) Must Be True
The correct answer here must be true. The remaining could all be false. Each answer lists an office that one employee *cannot* get. So, if the employee listed *could* get that office, the answer is wrong.

Jackson could choose office X if Paulson goes first and takes away Jackson's top choice of Y. That eliminates **(A)**.

Larabee could choose office W if Larabee goes last and everyone else chooses X, Y, and Z. That eliminates **(B)**.

Larabee could choose Z if Torillo goes first and takes away Larabee's top choice of X (as seen in the previous question). That eliminates **(C)**.

Torillo could certainly choose X if Torillo goes first. That eliminates **(D)**.

That leaves **(E)** as the correct answer. Sure enough, Paulson cannot select X, which is Paulson's third choice. That would require two employees to choose Y and Z before Paulson gets to choose X. However, Larabee and Torillo have X as a top choice. Even if Jackson went first and chose Y, Larabee or Torillo would go second and select X before Paulson gets the chance.

Game 4: Community Committee Volunteers

Step 1: Overview

Situation: Volunteers being assigned to a series of community committees

Entities: Five volunteers (Haddad, Joslin, Kwon, Molina, Nash), three committees (X, Y, Z), and three positions on each committee (leader, secretary, treasurer)

Action: Matching. Determine which volunteers are assigned to each committee and which position each volunteer holds on that committee.

Limitations: Each committee will consist of three volunteers, one for each of the three positions. That's a total of nine positions among three committees. With only five volunteers to choose from, some volunteers will be assigned to multiple committees. However, there is no minimum or maximum for each volunteer. Any volunteer can appear on one, two, or even all three committees.

(Note: Some may question whether every volunteer even has to be used. The overview never directly states that, although it can be argued that it's implied by the opening language: "Exactly five volunteers ... *are* being assigned." There have been games with entities that go unused, so it's wise to consider. However, Deductions in this game will make it impossible for anyone to be left out, so there is no penalty for overlooking that possibility here.)

Step 2: Sketch

Start by listing the volunteers by initial. Then, build a table with a column for each committee. In each column, there should be three slots: one for the leader, one for the secretary, and one for the treasurer. Keep all of the corresponding slots lined up and labeled for clear reference.

```
H J K M N
       x   y   z
lead  ___ ___ ___
secr  ___ ___ ___
trea  ___ ___ ___
```

Step 3: Rules

Rule 1 dictates that Nash be the leader of any committee to which Nash is assigned. While it's unknown which committees Nash will join, it is certain that Nash will never be a secretary or treasurer. Add "~ N" next to the secretary and treasurer rows.

Rule 2 limits Molina to one committee. That could be any of the three at this point, so add a "1" above M in the entity list to indicate this restriction.

Rule 3 establishes Kwon on Y, but not on Z. There's no indication what position Kwon will hold on Y. For now, add a "K" under column Y and "~ K" under column Z.

Rule 4 establishes Joslin as the secretary for Y, but prevents Joslin from being on X or Z. Add J to the appropriate slot in column Y, and add "~ J" under columns X and Z.

Step 4: Deductions

There are lots of deductions to be had in this game, so take some time to set as much up as possible. The key is to take negative information and turn it into positive information. Start with committee Z. By Rules 3 and 4, that committee cannot contain Kwon or Joslin. So, the three positions have to be filled by the remaining three volunteers: Haddad, Molina, and Nash. By Rule 1, Nash will be the leader. Haddad and Molina will be the secretary and treasurer, in either order.

With Molina on Z, Molina is done (Rule 2). That means Molina will not be on X or Y. By Rule 4, Joslin is not on X, either. Once again, that leaves three positions to be filled by the remaining volunteers: Haddad, Kwon, and Nash. Again, Nash will be the leader. Haddad and Kwon will be the secretary and treasurer, in either order.

That leaves committee Y. Joslin is the secretary (Rule 4), and Kwon will be either the leader or the treasurer (Rule 3). The remaining position belongs to either Haddad or Nash.

```
       x     y     z
lead │  N    ___   N
secr │ H/K   J    H/M
trea │ K/H   ___  M/H
             K
            H/N
```

Step 5: Questions

18. (E) Partial Acceptability

The correct answer will be one possible assignment of volunteers to Z. The four wrong answers will be unacceptable.

Z cannot contain Kwon (Rule 3) or Joslin (Rule 4), which eliminates **(A)**, **(B)**, and **(C)**. Nash can only be a leader (Rule 1). That eliminates **(D)**, making **(E)** the correct answer. The Master Sketch confirms this possible outcome.

19. (C) "If" / Could Be True EXCEPT

For this question, the one correct answer must be false and the four incorrect answers could be true. The new "If" says Kwon will be treasurer of two committees. Kwon cannot be assigned to Z (Rule 3), so Kwon will be treasurer of X and Y. By the Master Sketch, that means Haddad will be the secretary of X and either Haddad or Nash will be the leader of Y. The assignments for Z remain uncertain.

```
       x     y     z
lead │  N    H/N   N
secr │  H     J    H/M
trea │  K     K    M/H
```

With that, all of the answers are possible except for **(C)** because Kwon must be the treasurer for X. That makes **(C)** the correct answer.

20. (B) Must Be True EXCEPT

The four wrong answers to this question must be true no matter what. The correct answer might be possible, but could also be false.

Haddad could be assigned to Y, but Nash could be assigned to Y in lieu of Haddad. In that case, Y would consist of Nash as leader, Joslin as secretary, and Kwon as treasurer. Thus, Haddad does not have to be assigned to Y, making **(B)** the correct answer.

21. (B) "If" / Complete and Accurate List

For this question, Kwon is the leader of one committee. Nash is already the leader of X and Z, so Kwon will have to be the leader for Y. Joslin is the secretary for Y (Rule 4). That leaves Haddad or Nash to be treasurer, but Nash cannot be treasurer (Rule 1). So, Haddad is the treasurer of Y. No further deductions can be made to the other committees.

	x	y	z
lead	N	K	N
secr	H/K	J	H/M
trea	K/H	H	M/H

The question asks for a complete list of the committees that are entirely determined. That would be Y, and nothing else, making **(B)** the correct answer.

22. (C) Completely Determine

The correct answer to this question will make it possible to determine which volunteer is assigned to each position on each committee with complete certainty. The remaining answers will leave some uncertainty.

If Haddad was the leader for one committee, it would have to be Y. However, that would not help determine anything further about X or Z. That eliminates **(A)**.

If Haddad was the secretary of two committees, they would be X and Z. That would help determine the treasurer for those committees, too. However, that would leave Y open-ended, with Kwon still able to be leader or treasurer. That eliminates **(B)**.

If Haddad was the treasurer of all three committees, then Kwon would be the secretary for X and Molina would be secretary for Z. Kwon still needs a position on Y, so Kwon would be leader.

	x	y	z
lead	N	K	N
secr	K	J	M
trea	H	H	H

With everything complete, that makes **(C)** the correct answer. For the record:

If Kwon was treasurer of two committees (as seen in the second question of this game), they would be X and Y.

However, the leader of Y is still uncertain, as is the secretary and treasurer of Z. That eliminates **(D)**.

If Nash is the leader of all three committees, Kwon would have to be treasurer of Y. However, the secretary and treasurer positions of X and Z would still be uncertain. That eliminates **(E)**.

23. (C) Rule Substitution

For this question, Rule 2 is removed from the game. The correct answer will be a rule that could replace Rule 2 without changing anything from the original setup. In other words, it will reestablish the original rule without adding any new restrictions.

The original rule restricted Molina to one committee. Because Kwon and Joslin cannot be on Z (Rules 3 and 4), Molina will certainly be assigned to that one committee. The correct answer will prevent Molina from being assigned to any more committees, without further restricting anyone else.

Haddad and Nash could be on all three committees. Assigning either one to more committees than Molina would allow Molina to be on two committees. That eliminates **(A)** and **(E)**.

Joslin could only be on one committee (Rule 4). If Joslin was assigned more than Molina, Molina couldn't be on any committees, which would lead to an impossible scenario. That eliminates **(B)**.

Kwon can only be on two committees. If Kwon was assigned to more than Molina, Molina would be confined to one committee, just as the original rules intended. That makes **(C)** the correct answer. For the record:

By the deductions, Haddad is at least on Z. If Molina were on *more* committees, Molina would have to be on at least two, contrary to the original rules. That eliminates **(D)**.

Section IV: Logical Reasoning

Q#	Question Type	Correct	Difficulty
1	Principle (Identify/Strengthen)	A	★
2	Point at Issue	C	★
3	Paradox	E	★
4	Strengthen	B	★
5	Assumption (Sufficient)	A	★
6	Flaw	C	★
7	Role of a Statement	D	★
8	Main Point	A	★
9	Flaw	D	★
10	Inference	D	★★
11	Weaken	D	★★
12	Flaw	A	★★
13	Inference	D	★
14	Role of a Statement	E	★★★
15	Inference	C	★★
16	Role of a Statement	B	★★
17	Strengthen	B	★★
18	Inference	D	★★★★
19	Weaken	A	★★★★
20	Assumption (Sufficient)	B	★★★★
21	Paradox (EXCEPT)	B	★★
22	Role of a Statement	C	★★★
23	Parallel Reasoning	B	★★
24	Assumption (Sufficient)	D	★
25	Parallel Flaw	B	★★
26	Assumption (Necessary)	E	★★★

1. (A) Principle (Identify/Strengthen)

Step 1: Identify the Question Type

The question directly asks for a principle, one that will "justify" the reasoning provided. That means it is an Identify the Principle question that will require the same skills as a Strengthen question.

Step 2: Untangle the Stimulus

The pundit is arguing that Grenier probably won't be elected mayor. As evidence, the pundit points out how Grenier has changed her position on wages and now voters see her as insincere.

Step 3: Make a Prediction

The pundit's prediction about Grenier's electability hinges entirely on voters' perception of insincerity. For this argument to work, Grenier must be acting on the principle that the appearance of insincerity will affect the way people vote.

Step 4: Evaluate the Answer Choices

(A) matches the principle, connecting insincerity to people's voting habits.

(B) is a 180. The fact that people view Grenier as insincere is a pretty good sign that they *did* notice her change in stance.

(C) is Out of Scope. It's not about voters *agreeing* with Grenier, it's about them viewing Grenier as insincere.

(D) is Out of Scope. The voters' financial concerns are not an issue here. It's all about Grenier's flip-flopping.

(E) is Out of Scope. The pundit never mentions what beliefs the voters have, and this does nothing to justify the conclusion about Grenier being elected.

2. (C) Point at Issue

Step 1: Identify the Question Type

The stimulus provides arguments by two speakers, and the question asks for something over which they "disagree." That makes this a Point at Issue question.

Step 2: Untangle the Stimulus

Albert condemns Swenson's book as poor scholarship, but argues that it still has some value in that it encourages further research. Yvonne uses an analogy to counter Albert: saying the book has value is the same as saying a virus has value because it encourages epidemiologists.

Step 3: Make a Prediction

Sure, viruses might give epidemiologists something to think about, but it's hard to argue that viruses are really valuable. That's the argument Yvonne is making about Swenson's book: it might encourage a few people to think about sun exposure, but that doesn't make it valuable. And that's the

point at issue: Albert finds value in the book, while Yvonne finds none.

Step 4: Evaluate the Answer Choices

(C) is correct. Albert believes it *should* be considered valuable, while Yvonne feels it *shouldn't*.

(A) is only mentioned in Albert's argument. Yvonne offers no argument against that claim.

(B) is a 180. Despite the value Albert finds in the book, he does admit it's poor scholarship, and Yvonne is all too likely to agree with that claim.

(D) is a Distortion. Yvonne does not argue that the book *didn't* spur new research. She merely argues that such encouragement is not enough to consider the book valuable.

(E) is Out of Scope. All that's stated is that Swenson's book *did* stimulate new research. Neither Albert nor Yvonne addresses books that do *not* stimulate new research.

3. (E) Paradox

Step 1: Identify the Question Type

The question asks for something that will "explain" a "surprising finding." That makes this a Paradox question.

Step 2: Untangle the Stimulus

According to the researchers, people in countries with high income are more likely to become entrepreneurs than people in countries with moderate income, which makes sense because high-income countries offer more business opportunities. Somehow, though, people in *low*-income countries are even *more* likely to start new businesses.

Step 3: Make a Prediction

Using the researcher's reasoning, the high-income countries have the most business opportunities, which should make them the most likely to experience new businesses. So, why are the low-income countries, with theoretically the *fewest* business opportunities, experiencing an even higher rate of new businesses? The correct answer will provide a significant difference to low-income countries that encourages people to start new businesses despite the lack of opportunities.

Step 4: Evaluate the Answer Choices

(E) provides an explanation. It's precisely *because* of the lack of business opportunities that people in low-income countries start their own businesses; there are no other viable options. So, instead of settling for a terrible job or unemployment, they're forced to create their own business.

(A) is an Irrelevant Comparison. The number of employees in new business doesn't help explain *why* citizens of low-income countries are starting such businesses while lacking opportunities.

(B) is a 180. This gives citizens of low-income countries even *less* incentive and *less* assistance, which makes it even harder to understand why they're taking so many risks on new businesses.

(C) is a 180. If businesses in low-income countries were more likely to succeed, then *that* might explain why so many citizens there are taking the risk. However, with equal success rates, the question remains why they're starting new businesses in the face of little opportunity.

(D) just refers to the disillusion faced by entrepreneurs in high-income countries. However, there's no reason to believe that entrepreneurs in low-income countries would be any different, which means the mystery goes unresolved.

4. (B) Strengthen

Step 1: Identify the Question Type

The question asks for something that will "support," or Strengthen, the given argument.

Step 2: Untangle the Stimulus

People avoided a particular film, and its director argues that this was not because of a few negative reviews. As evidence, the director suggests that her films have small audiences to begin with, and those people had other similar films to choose from that weekend.

Step 3: Make a Prediction

The director overlooks an alternative solution for audiences: If they wanted to, they could just go out and see all the movies that interested them. If people had the option of seeing multiple movies, then perhaps they *did* avoid the director's film because of the reviews. Removing that possibility would help the director's cause.

Step 4: Evaluate the Answer Choices

(B) helps the director's defense. By limiting themselves to one movie, filmgoers were split, meaning reduced audiences for all films—regardless of what the reviews said.

(A) is a 180. If the one or two negative reviews were the *only* reviews, and *nobody* reviewed the film positively, then that is more likely to be the reason people shunned the film.

(C) is a 180. In this case, negative reviews could still explain why people shunned the movie despite more people seeing movies overall.

(D) is a 180. If other films received positive reviews while the director's film received negative reviews, this makes it *more* likely that the reviews were responsible.

(E) is irrelevant. The director admits that the number of viewers for her films is already "relatively small," so the movie choices of most people has no effect on why *her* usual audience members stayed away.

5. (A) Assumption (Sufficient)

Step 1: Identify the Question Type

The question asks for something that would help the argument reach its conclusion. The blank in the argument is preceded by the Keyword *since*. That means the blank will be filled in with a missing piece of evidence, which is the definition of an assumption.

Step 2: Untangle the Stimulus

Despite how complex some scientific issues are, readers are often fascinated by stories about those issues. Unfortunately, the author argues that popular magazines won't cover those issues very often.

Step 3: Make a Prediction

If readers are so fascinated by these stories, why not cover them? The only evidence given is that the stories are too complex and readers of popular magazines struggle to understand them. The author must assume that such challenges override public interest when it comes to deciding what popular magazines cover.

Step 4: Evaluate the Answer Choices

(A) is a match. If editors base their decision on how likely a story is to be understood, that would make it clear why popular magazines are leaving out these complex stories despite the public interest.

(B) is a 180. If a magazine's success depends on appealing to readers, then it makes no sense for a magazine to leave out such fascinating stories.

(C) is irrelevant. How common such issues are does nothing to explain why magazines would leave them out.

(D) is irrelevant. Making readers unable to determine how much they really understand does nothing to further the magazine's decision to not cover these stories.

(E) is irrelevant. Even if people don't actively seek out such articles, that doesn't explain why popular magazines won't at least try to appeal to their readers' fascination.

6. (C) Flaw

Step 1: Identify the Question Type

The question asks why the given argument is "vulnerable to criticism," which means it is asking for the flaw in the argument.

Step 2: Untangle the Stimulus

The author is refuting the newspaper's claim that it covers the most popular high school sports. As evidence, the author cites that track is more popular in the school than basketball, yet the newspaper covers basketball and not track.

Step 3: Make a Prediction

This is a classic case of equivocation—equating two different ideas merely because they are expressed by the same word. In this case, when the author says track is more popular than basketball, *popular* refers to how many students *participate* in a sport. When the newspaper uses the term, *popular* refers to how interested people are in *reading about* the sport. Even though fewer students play basketball, basketball could still be a more popular sport among readers. The correct answer will point out this confusion.

Step 4: Evaluate the Answer Choices

(C) is correct. The author misinterprets the meaning of *popular*, thinking it only refers to the number of students who play a given sport.

(A) is Out of Scope. The author makes no claim about one thing causing another.

(B) is a Distortion. The statistics only refer to 20 percent of the school population, but the numbers are substantial enough to confirm the author's comparison between track and basketball. There's no flaw there. The flaw comes when the author uses this comparison to argue a claim about popularity among the newspaper's readers.

(D) refers to circular reasoning (using evidence that merely restates the conclusion), but that's not the case here. The evidence and the conclusion are adequately distinct.

(E) is a 180. This not an ad hominem attack. The author uses statistical evidence to back up the conclusion, which only attacks the newspaper's claim, not the newspaper itself.

7. (D) Role of a Statement

Step 1: Identify the Question Type

The question cites a claim from the stimulus and asks for its "role in the argument." That makes this a Role of a Statement question.

Step 2: Untangle the Stimulus

Most people feel it's environmentally friendly to buy food from local farmers. The author argues otherwise. While transportation concerns are valid, some distant locations may have production practices that are more environmentally friendly and can thus be preferable overall.

Step 3: Make a Prediction

The claim in question is in the very first sentence, presented as something "widely believed." Once the author uses the Keyword *But*, it's clear the author is not convinced. By the conclusion, the author expresses the exact opposite of that opening belief: buying local food is *not* always the best choice. The correct answer will identify the opening claim as a mere belief, and one that the author refutes.

Step 4: Evaluate the Answer Choices

(D) is correct.

(A) is a Distortion. The argument is not *based* on the claim in question; it's designed to *refute* that claim.

(B) is a Distortion. While the claim does support buying local foods, this answer ignores the rest of the argument in which the author does *not* support that activity.

(C) is a Distortion. While the author ultimately suggests buying local foods is not always the best idea, the claim in question does not itself provide reason for that rejection.

(E) is a Distortion. The claim in question is "widely believed," which means it's a point *others* might argue. However, the author's conclusion argues the opposite of this claim.

8. (A) Main Point

Step 1: Identify the Question Type

The question asks for the *conclusion* of the argument, making this a Main Point question.

Step 2: Untangle the Stimulus

This author is praising technology for improving our lives, and not just for its direct effects. It has indirectly helped the growth of many businesses (design, production, testing, etc.), which helps increase economic and spiritual well-being.

Step 3: Make a Prediction

The phrase "After all" is used to indicate evidence for the sentence before it. In this case, the second sentence about the growth of various industries is evidence to support the first sentence that technology is not just helping people via direct application. The final sentence regarding the effect on jobs, taxes, and renewal is just further support for the claim in the first sentence. Thus, the main point is that first sentence: technology is improving our lives, and not just directly.

Step 4: Evaluate the Answer Choices

(A) summarizes the main point perfectly, praising technology and not just for its direct applications.

(B) is evidence, not the conclusion.

(C) is from the last sentence, but that's just further evidence for the conclusion that technology is improving our lives.

(D) is a Distortion. The author doesn't claim that it's either creation *or* direct application that's helping, and the last two sentences list more reasons than that (including testing and marketing).

(E) is Extreme. While this accurately expresses some of the ways in which technology is helping, these are not the *only* ways. The author suggests that these are ways *in addition* to direct application, as mentioned in the first sentence.

9. (D) Flaw

Step 1: Identify the Question Type

The question asks why the given argument is "vulnerable to criticism," which is a common way for asking for the flaw in the argument.

Step 2: Untangle the Stimulus

The author argues that Joshi's votes are being swayed by campaign contributions. As evidence, the author cites Joshi's sizable contributions from property developers as well as Joshi's frequent votes that benefit property developers.

Step 3: Make a Prediction

It would be easy to claim the flaw of Correlation vs. Causation here. Joshi's votes do line up conveniently with the interest of his supporters (correlation), but it's not logically proper to conclude that his votes were *influenced* by those contributions (causation). However, there's more to this story. The contributions are for Joshi's *reelection*, which means Joshi was already city councillor and probably voted before he even needed those contributions. So, even if there *is* causality, the author likely has it backwards: maybe it's his pro-developer votes that influenced the contributions and not the other way around.

Step 4: Evaluate the Answer Choices

(D) points out the author's error. The author assumes that large contributions were the cause of Joshi's actions when it really could be the other way around: large contributions are the *result* of his actions.

(A) is a clever Distortion. While this does raise the question of Correlation vs. Causation, this states the author assumes that the "earlier events" were the cause. However, the author argues that large contributions are the cause of Joshi's voting behavior, but there's no evidence that contributions were made *before* Joshi voted.

(B) raises a common flaw, but one that has no bearing here. The author makes no mention of anything that's "necessary."

(C) is Out of Scope. The author never broaches the subject of morality.

(E) suggests circular reasoning. However, the evidence describes correlated events, and the conclusion implies causality. Those are distinct ideas, and not merely a repetition of one another.

10. (D) Inference

Step 1: Identify the Question Type

For this question, the given information will "provide reason" for choosing the correct answer, which makes this an Inference question. However, unlike most Inference questions, the correct answer here will be the one that will be "reject[ed]" by the information provided. In other words, the correct answer will be the one that is false.

Step 2: Untangle the Stimulus

Some people say that government can't manage financial institutions and thus shouldn't take over failing banks. *However*, the columnist argues against that claim, saying that government wouldn't actually *run* the banks it takes over. The government would assign new managers who know what they're doing, similar to how politicians with little military experience staff the defense department with proper officials who know what they're doing.

Step 3: Make a Prediction

The gist of the columnist's argument is that it's okay for government to take over failing banks. The day-to-day business will be handled just fine by proper managers, not the government itself. The correct answer will be contradictory to these points.

Step 4: Evaluate the Answer Choices

(D) is the correct answer. The columnist states that, even though the government would *own* the bank, it wouldn't actually *manage* the bank. That would be done by qualified managers, just like our military is managed by top appointed officials. So, such banks *can* be well managed.

(A) is Out of Scope. The columnist doesn't mention the knowledge needed for either job, so this answer couldn't be rejected.

(B) is a 180. The use of the analogy suggests that politicians certainly *are* doing a fine job in selecting military officials. That's why the columnist contradicts people who believe government couldn't manage banks as well.

(C) is Out of Scope and potentially a 180. The columnist never says anything about politicians running the bank. Besides, the columnist states that government would *not* manage day-to-day operations, supporting (and not rejecting) this idea that politicians are not right for the job.

(E) is Out of Scope. The argument is about taking over failed banks, not sound ones. It's perfectly possible that the columnist would agree with (and not reject) government leaving sound banks alone.

11. (D) Weaken

Step 1: Identify the Question Type

The question directly asks for something that weakens the given argument.

Step 2: Untangle the Stimulus

The author cites polls of university students in which graduating students are more likely to be against reducing social services than first-year students. The author uses this to conclude that university graduates would favor increased social services more than the overall population.

Step 3: Make a Prediction

This is a classic case of faulty representativeness. The poll only involves *students*, yet the author dares to apply the findings to all "people with a university education" and the "overall population." This sweeping generalization requires two assumptions: 1) The views of graduating students represent the views of anyone with a university education. 2) The views of students overall represent that of the overall population. Any answer that contradicts one of these assumptions will weaken the argument.

Step 4: Evaluate the Answer Choices

(D) weakens the argument by questioning a major assumption. The views of today's graduating students don't necessarily reflect the views of all past graduates. If so many past graduates favor *reduced* social services, that would contradict the author's belief.

(A) is a 180. This suggests that the polls were done carefully to avoid error, giving further credence to the author's argument.

(B) is a 180. This just provides reasoning *why* university graduates would favor increased services, which would only support the author's belief.

(C) is a 180. Ignoring the "retired" part, this just compares graduates to nongraduates, and graduates are less likely to favor reductions. That makes graduates more likely to favor *increases*, exactly as the author claims.

(E) is a 180. If the graduating students have stronger opinions, they'd be less likely to change their minds. The other students would be *more* likely to change their minds, eventually making pro-social service a majority opinion among graduates.

12. (A) Flaw

Step 1: Identify the Question Type

The question directly asks why the argument is flawed.

Step 2: Untangle the Stimulus

Some critics claim a particular movie will encourage bad behavior, but the author claims that view is based on a flawed survey. Thus, the author concludes that the critics are wrong.

Step 3: Make a Prediction

This is a common error on the LSAT. Yes, the survey cited was flawed. However, even if the survey was flawed, the critics' opinion could still be valid for *other* reasons. Bad evidence does not imply a bad conclusion.

Step 4: Evaluate the Answer Choices

(A) describes this classic flaw. The author infers that the critics are wrong just because their evidence is unsatisfactory (i.e., the survey was flawed).

(B) is Out of Scope. The only claim provided is one the author claims is false. There is no pejorative (i.e., disparaging) claim that's true to make such a comparison.

(C) is not a flaw here. The author doesn't rely on a sample; the author merely relies on evidence that a particular survey is flawed.

(D) is incorrect. The author *does* attack the critics' argument by attacking the study they use to support their claim. The author makes no attack on the critics themselves.

(E) gets the logic backwards. The author fails to consider that, even though their *evidence* is faulty, the critics' *conclusion* may still be true … not the other way around.

13. (D) Inference

Step 1: Identify the Question Type

The correct answer "must … be true" based on the information given, making this an Inference question.

Step 2: Untangle the Stimulus

The information is clear: most skilled banjo players are skilled guitar players, but not the other way around.

Step 3: Make a Prediction

Some sample numbers could help clear this up. Say there are 100 banjo players. In that case, at least 51 of them are also good guitar players. However, that overlap group of 51 people does *not* represent most guitar players. So, there must be more guitar players (say 500) than banjo players.

Step 4: Evaluate the Answer Choices

(D) must be true. After all, if there were an equal number of guitar and banjo players, then a majority overlap would be a majority overlap for *both* groups, not just one.

(A) could be true, but need not be. There could be millions of skilled guitar players who are not good at the banjo, yet only a couple of hundred skilled banjo players.

(B) is Out of Scope. There's nothing in the stimulus about success rates—only the number of people who have the skills.

(C) is Out of Scope. The stimulus only provides information about numbers, not what skills are required.

(E) is a 180. If there were more banjo players, and most of them were good guitar players, then it wouldn't be possible for most guitar players to be unable to play banjo. (To illustrate, if there were 100 banjo players, and most were good guitar players, at least 51 would be good at both. With

99 guitar players total or less, 51 players who could also play banjo would automatically be a majority, too.)

14. (E) Role of a Statement

Step 1: Identify the Question Type

This question provides a claim from the stimulus and asks for its "role" in the argument, making this a Role of a Statement question.

Step 2: Untangle the Stimulus

To start a company, one does need entrepreneurial abilities, but can also fail without proper management skills (e.g., ability to analyze trends). Hence, the author concludes that *both* entrepreneurial and management skills are important.

Step 3: Make a Prediction

The claim in question is part of the third sentence, which begins "For instance." That indicates it's part of the example used to support the claim before it: some companies fail due to a lack of managerial skills. That claim, in turn, is used to support the author's final conclusion (indicated by *Hence*) that success depends on both entrepreneurial and management skills. The correct answer will describe this two-phase function: the claim is an example to support a point that is ultimately used to support the main conclusion.

Step 4: Evaluate the Answer Choices

(E) is a match.

(A) is not accurate. The conclusion is the last sentence, not the claim in question.

(B) is a Distortion. The author's argument is not designed to explain anything.

(C) is a 180. It's a significant example that justifies the author's primary piece of evidence. While the argument could potentially function without it, it still serves as much more than a mere side note.

(D) is inaccurate. The conclusion does not mention company growth. Instead, the claim about company growth leads *indirectly* to the conclusion by supporting the claim about the need for managerial skills.

15. (C) Inference

Step 1: Identify the Question Type

The correct answer will be "supported by the information" given, making this an Inference question.

Step 2: Untangle the Stimulus

The author dismisses the efforts of outsiders bringing fresh ideas to a field. The author claims that solving problems requires understanding, which in turn requires experience.

Step 3: Make a Prediction

Notice the very strong language in the last sentence. *Only* people with understanding can solve problems, and *no one* gets that understanding without experience. So, by that logic, anyone without experience in a field will be unable to solve problems in that field. Alternatively, by contrapositive, if someone *does* come up with a solution, that person *must* have experience in that field.

Step 4: Evaluate the Answer Choices

(C) is logically deducible from the last sentence. All solutions, creative or otherwise, must come from someone with experience.

(A) is a Distortion. The author never correlates experience with creativity.

(B) is a Distortion. Experience is said to be necessary for coming up with solutions, not sufficient. It's possible that most people have the experience but are *still* unable to find solutions.

(D) is Out of Scope. The author makes no mention of variation among different levels of complexity.

(E) is Extreme. While outsiders will be incapable of devising solutions to problems, that doesn't mean they should be denied *any* responsibility without training.

16. (B) Role of a Statement

Step 1: Identify the Question Type

The question provides a claim from the stimulus and asks for its "role" in the argument. That makes this a Role of a Statement question.

Step 2: Untangle the Stimulus

According to the researcher, dinosaurs lack a feature usually found in warm-blooded creatures. Some believe that makes dinosaurs cold-blooded, but the researcher disagrees. Some dinosaurs were discovered in areas where cold-blooded animals couldn't survive.

Step 3: Make a Prediction

The claim in question is the last sentence. However, that's not the conclusion. This argument has the common structure of presenting a point of view and rejecting it. The author's conclusion is that paleobiologists are wrong, and there *were* warm-blooded dinosaurs. The claim in question, that only warm-blooded animals could survive in the area where certain dinosaurs lived, is the author's evidence in support of that conclusion.

Step 4: Evaluate the Answer Choices

(B) correctly identifies the last sentence as supporting evidence.

(A) is a 180. The last sentence *supports* the author's conclusion.

(C) is a Distortion. While it certainly contradicts the claim that all dinosaurs are cold-blooded, it doesn't negate the claim about the missing turbinates.

(D) is incorrect. The author's conclusion is that the paleobiologists are mistaken.

(E) is a Distortion. The existence of dinosaurs in Australia and Alaska is not support for *why* warm-blooded animals can't survive there.

17. (B) Strengthen

Step 1: Identify the Question Type

The question asks for something that will "justify" the given application, which makes this a Strengthen question. This is a variation that involves a principle and a specific situation that supposedly applies that principle. The application usually leaves something out from the principle, and the correct answer will add the missing piece.

Step 2: Untangle the Stimulus

The principle is that government should always allow people to express their beliefs, as long as expressing that belief isn't harmful to others. The application states that government shouldn't have repressed Calista from expressing her belief about the link between cell phones and cancer.

Step 3: Make a Prediction

The problem with the application is that the principle doesn't entirely allow *all* beliefs to be expressed. There are possible exceptions, namely beliefs that could be harmful to people. To completely match the principle, it's important to know that Calista's view isn't an exception. In other words, the correct answer needs to confirm that Calista's views aren't harmful to others.

Step 4: Evaluate the Answer Choices

(B) fills in the final piece. By confirming that Calista's beliefs are valid and can actually *help* people, her beliefs don't meet the exception of the principle and thus should not be repressed, just as the application concludes.

(A) is not enough because it doesn't reveal the results of the research. If they found no link, then Calista's beliefs *could* be harmful to people, and the principle would allow for repression.

(C) is a Distortion. It doesn't matter if she *believes* people won't be harmed. It's whether or not people are actually going to *be* unharmed that determines whether the principle applies.

(D) could be a 180. It's unknown if Calista's evidence is strong or not, and if it's not, this suggests that her beliefs could be

harmful. In that case, the application could be wrong as the principle would allow for repression.

(E) depends on people being convinced. Without knowing that for sure, it's still unsure if Calista's views are harmful or not. Thus, it can't be determined if the principle properly applies or not.

18. (D) Inference

Step 1: Identify the Question Type

The question asks for something that can be "properly inferred" from the given information, which makes this an Inference question.

Step 2: Untangle the Stimulus

Reading an alphabetic language requires two things: phonemic awareness and learning how sounds are symbolized by letters. Many kids have learned to read an alphabetic language despite learning a method called "whole-language," which emphasizes the way words sound.

Step 3: Make a Prediction

The whole-language method is said to emphasize the way words sound, which fits the concept of phonemic awareness (knowing that language can be broken into sounds). However, kids learning from this method are said to be able to read alphabetic languages. By the second claim, that would require learning how sounds are represented by letters. So, it must be true that those kids were able to learn how sounds are represented by letters.

Step 4: Evaluate the Answer Choices

(D) must be true. By the second claim, because there are kids taught the whole-language method that *can* read alphabetic languages, those kids must have been able to learn how letters represent sounds.

(A) is Extreme. The stimulus only talks about what "many" children were able to do. There's no evidence that the whole-language method "invariably succeeds" at anything.

(B) is Extreme. This happened for "many" children, but it's not assured this will happen.

(C) is an Extreme Distortion. Phonemic awareness and knowledge of how sounds are represented are *necessary*, but some people can have both skills and still be unable to read alphabetic languages. And even if someone *was* unable to read such a language, they could still have one skill and not the other. They wouldn't have to be missing *both*.

(E) is a Distortion. Those students who did learn to read alphabetic languages must have learned how to represent sounds symbolically, but there's no evidence that they learned that from the whole-language method. They could have learned a second method that gave them that knowledge.

19. (A) Weaken

Step 1: Identify the Question Type

The question asks for something that "undermines" the argument, which is common LSAT language for a Weaken question.

Step 2: Untangle the Stimulus

According to studies, more pedestrians get hit by a car when using crosswalks than when not using them. The author argues this is due to a false sense of security. People think they're automatically safer in crosswalks and are less likely to look both ways before crossing.

Step 3: Make a Prediction

The author provides one reasonable explanation, but overlooks any other reason why more people are getting hit within the crosswalk. Similar arguments have appeared numerous times on the LSAT, and the author always makes the same assumption: that an equal number of people do both activities (i.e., an equal number use the crosswalk as don't use it). However, if a lot more people use the crosswalk, there's just more opportunity there for an accident. It's pure statistics. The author would have less reason to bring up the sense of security.

Step 4: Evaluate the Answer Choices

(A) is the common weakener to this kind of argument.

(B) is irrelevant. An increase in incidents overall doesn't change the author's explanation for why more such incidents happen *in* the crosswalk rather than *out*.

(C) is a 180. This strengthens the author's contention that people have a false sense of security. They just trust the crosswalk signals and don't bother looking at the traffic themselves.

(D) is a 180. If drivers are more alert at crosswalks, then it's more likely the cause of the problem has to do with the pedestrians—exactly what the author is contending.

(E) is a 180. This says that safety measures (e.g., crosswalks) make people less cautious, which is pretty much exactly what the author is claiming.

20. (B) Assumption (Sufficient)

Step 1: Identify the Question Type

The correct answer will complete the argument "if" it is "assumed." That makes this a Sufficient Assumption question.

Step 2: Untangle the Stimulus

Selena claims to be psychic. The author concludes that determining the validity of her claim will provide proof if psychic powers really exist.

Step 3: Make a Prediction

The author argues that knowing whether Selena's claim is true or not will confirm the possibility of psychic powers. In other words, if Selena *does* have psychic powers, then they exist. If Selena does *not* have psychic powers, then they do *not* exist.

| If | Selena is psychic | → | possible |
| If | Selena ~ psychic | → | ~ possible |

The first claim is logically sound. If Selena has psychic powers, then *of course* they exist. However, what if Selena is *not* psychic? The author offers no evidence that psychic powers would be impossible for anyone else. For this argument to be valid, the author is assuming that that is the case.

Step 4: Evaluate the Answer Choices

(B) is correct. This says that Selena *must* have psychic powers to prove their existence. If she doesn't, then they don't exist—and it's logical to say that if she *does* have such powers, then they *do* exist. Put those two together, and the author's conclusion is confirmed: whether Selena has such powers will determine whether they exist.

(A) is a Distortion. If Selena was found to be *not* psychic, this answer still wouldn't confirm or deny the existence of psychic powers. It would still be possible that psychic ability has just yet to be discovered.

(C) is not good enough. Even if it *were* possible to determine Selena's ability for sure, what would happen if it was determined that she was *wrong* and wasn't psychic? The argument would still be unconvincing because perhaps somebody *else* could be psychic.

(D) is a 180. This suggests that finding out Selena's claim is false would lead to uncertainty. The author argues that a conclusion would be certain either way—whether Selena's claim is true or not.

(E) is an Extreme Distortion. The author says *if* we find out about Selena's claim, then that will be good enough. This answer makes it *necessary* to find out about her claim, which is the wrong Formal Logic. There could be other ways to confirm the existence of psychic powers (e.g., proving someone *else* has them).

21. (B) Paradox (EXCEPT)

Step 1: Identify the Question Type

The question asks for something that would "explain the situation described." That makes this a Paradox question. The EXCEPT indicates that four answers will resolve the central mystery. The correct answer will be the one that does *not* explain the mystery or makes it even more mysterious.

Step 2: Untangle the Stimulus

Researchers looked at prices for 300 common drugs sold in bulk at wholesalers. While there are suggested prices for these drugs in a price guidebook, researchers found the drugs being sold for far less.

Step 3: Make a Prediction

The mystery here is: why are bulk wholesalers selling these drugs at such a big discount? There could be many reasons, so don't try to predict exactly what the answers will say. Just note a few things. First, the research only involves wholesalers that sell in bulk. So, it's likely that some answers will address something unique about wholesalers or bulk sales that make them amenable to discounts. Also, the research involves only *common* drugs, so that could also factor into the explanation. Remember that one answer will not help explain the low prices, and that will be the correct answer.

Step 4: Evaluate the Answer Choices

(B) is the correct answer. If anything, this makes the mystery even weirder. If the guide recommends prices that are *already* relatively low, why are wholesalers reducing that price even more? There's still no good explanation.

(A) helps explain. The lower prices are being caused by wholesalers trying to outprice their competitors.

(C) helps explain. If the prices fluctuate, researchers might have just stopped by when prices hit a low (perhaps a big sale). Maybe the next month would have seen prices closer to the recommendations.

(D) helps explain. If the recommended prices are already so high as to guarantee "substantial profits," then wholesalers could slash prices as noted and *still* make some profit.

(E) helps explain. Perhaps selling the drugs in bulk is significantly more cost-effective and allows for prices substantially lower than those for smaller quantities.

22. (C) Role of a Statement

Step 1: Identify the Question Type

The question presents a claim from the stimulus and asks for its "role in the ... argument." That makes this a Role of a Statement question.

Step 2: Untangle the Stimulus

The theorist lists a few pairs of emotions (e.g., hatred and anger) that share a core emotion but are impossible to tell apart without a social and behavioral context. So, the theorist concludes that music can only produce the core of an emotion because it provides no definitive social or behavioral context.

Step 3: Make a Prediction

The claim in question ("music is merely sound") is preceded by the word *for*, which indicates that it is evidence for the claim before it. The claim it's supporting ("music produces [only] the core of a given emotion") is the author's main conclusion. The claim in question is also followed by the word *and*, which indicates that it is followed by yet another piece of evidence. So, the correct answer will identify the claim in question as part of the evidence in support of the conclusion.

Step 4: Evaluate the Answer Choices

(C) is correct.

(A) commits multiple errors. First, there is no "particular instance" cited of music producing only sound. Second, the claim doesn't undermine anything. Third, the author is not "attacking" any argument.

(B) is inaccurate. The word *for* immediately before the claim identifies it as evidence, not part of the conclusion.

(D) is Extreme. The author never claims that it's *necessary* for music to be merely sound.

(E) is a 180. This is a central piece of evidence. The author wouldn't reject it at all.

23. (B) Parallel Reasoning

Step 1: Identify the Question Type

The question asks for an answer with an argument "similar in its reasoning" to the one in the stimulus. That makes this a Parallel Reasoning question.

Step 2: Untangle the Stimulus

To be intelligent, a computer needs at least one of three things. A particular computer (AR3000) is missing two of those things. So, if it's intelligent, it must have the third.

Step 3: Make a Prediction

The structure is pretty clean. An entity (computers) fits a category (intelligent) only if it has one of three qualities (creativity, self-awareness, ability to learn from mistakes). A particular entity (AR3000) is missing two of those qualities, so it must have the third quality to fit the category. The correct answer will fit this structure exactly.

Step 4: Evaluate the Answer Choices

(B) matches piece by piece. An entity (vaccines) fits a category (commonly used) only if it has one of three qualities (dead-virus, attenuated-virus, or pure DNA). A particular entity (Vaccine X) is missing two of those qualities, so it must have the third quality to fit the category.

(A) is close, but applies the logic to all members of a set of entities ("Every vaccine") rather than saying what's needed to fit a particular category (e.g., for a computer to be intelligent or for the vaccine to be commonly used—as the correct answer states).

(C) also applies the logic to all members of a set of entities ("Every vaccine") rather than saying what's needed to fit a particular category (e.g., for a computer to be intelligent or for the vaccine to be commonly used—as the correct answer states).

(D) only states that the specific virus is missing *one* of the three qualities. The conclusion is conditional, claiming the third quality exists *if* the second one is missing. The original argument had no such conditional.

(E) only states that the specific virus is missing *one* of the three qualities. The conclusion is conditional, claiming the third quality exists *if* the second one is missing. The original argument had no such conditional.

24. (D) Assumption (Sufficient)

Step 1: Identify the Question Type

The correct answer will complete the argument "if" it is "assumed." That makes this a Sufficient Assumption question.

Step 2: Untangle the Stimulus

Mallotech claims to be socially responsible, but critics raise concerns about unsanitary working conditions. If those critics are right, the author argues that Mallotech's claim is rubbish.

Step 3: Make a Prediction

If the critics are right, then Mallotech has unsanitary working conditions. However, Mallotech is merely claiming to be "socially responsible," a concept neither the critics nor the author directly addresses. How do unsanitary conditions relate to social responsibility? The author assumes that there's a connection, and the correct answer will make that connection.

Step 4: Evaluate the Answer Choices

(D) is correct. If this were true and Mallotech *did* have unsanitary working conditions, then the author is justified in saying Mallotech is not really socially responsible.

(A) is Out of Scope. There's no evidence that Mallotech is lying about anything.

(B) is Out of Scope. There's nothing in the argument about Mallotech concealing information.

(C) adds nothing to the argument. It's already acknowledged that "many" factories are unsanitary, which would imply it affects many employees. The author still makes no connection between such working conditions and the concept of social responsibility.

(E) is Out of Scope. There's no evidence that unsanitary conditions indicate poor management. Even if they did, this

answer only mentions "well managed" companies. It would still be possible for poorly managed companies to be socially responsible, too.

25. (B) Parallel Flaw

Step 1: Identify the Question Type

The correct answer will be an argument "similar to" the given argument. In addition, the reasoning will be "flawed." That makes this a Parallel Flaw question. Remember that the correct answer must contain the exact same flaw as the original argument.

Step 2: Untangle the Stimulus

The author talks about dichotomous concepts—two ideas that are wholly distinct (e.g., right and wrong). However, the author then cites some pairs that are no longer considered dichotomous (e.g., plants and animals are no longer considered distinct—some things are considered *both*!). Therefore, the author recommends dropping the notion of dichotomous concepts altogether.

Step 3: Make a Prediction

That's rather drastic. A couple of examples become invalid, and the author suddenly wants to scrap *everything*. Isn't it possible that the general idea is still valid even if some exceptions have arisen? The correct answer will contain the same flaw: dismissing an entire concept because of a handful of exceptional cases.

Step 4: Evaluate the Answer Choices

(B) commits the same flaw. In this case, the author wants to dismiss *all* anti-anxiety drugs just because a few bad ones were found.

(A) does not match. The original argument contained a conclusion about eliminating something entirely. Here, such an elimination is part of the evidence to support a conclusion about some computers.

(C) is not flawed the same way. Here, the evidence and the conclusion are both about "all intoxicated drivers." The conclusion is not based on just a handful of bad instances.

(D) does not match. The author is not using exceptional cases. This argument is based on a relationship (the longer it's kept, the more likely it's rotten). The original contained no such relationship.

(E) mentions eliminating something because it doesn't match an assumption. That's not the same as eliminating something due to the existence of a few bad examples.

26. (E) Assumption (Necessary)

Step 1: Identify the Question Type

The question asks for an "assumption" that the argument "requires." That makes this a Necessary Assumption question.

Step 2: Untangle the Stimulus

The author is discussing ballast tanks that are used to keep ships stable. As ballast tanks are filled and emptied at port, local sea creatures can get into the tanks. They can then get out when the ship reaches another port, causing major problems in their new environment. So, the author offers a solution: when the ship is midocean, take a moment to drain the tanks and refill them. Any coastal stowaways that are drained out will not be able to survive. Any midocean creatures that climb aboard will not survive when drained out at port.

Step 3: Make a Prediction

While the author's plan spells doom for any creature that finds its way into a ballast tank, it seems like it would prevent ecological disasters caused by creatures invading a new environment. The problem is that the author calls the plan "viable." Unfortunately, some plans look good in theory but don't quite work out in practice. The author is overlooking any potential glitches in the plan. For this argument to work, the author must assume that everything will work out as planned, and nothing significant will go wrong.

Step 4: Evaluate the Answer Choices

(E) must be true. The whole point of the ballast tank is to help maintain stability. If draining the tanks midocean causes a problem and the ship becomes unstable, then the author's plan would put the ship and its crew at great risk. The plan would suddenly seem less viable. So, for the plan to work, it *must* be true that ships can stay stable while going through the "drain and refill" process.

(A) is Extreme. Remember that the correct answer must be one the argument "requires." While this answer would certainly be helpful to the author's cause, it's not entirely necessary. The proposal would not have to *ensure* that *no* harmful creatures are pumped into the tank. It could merely make that scenario *less likely* and still be considered viable.

(B) is a 180. For the plan to be viable, it would be best if the "drain and refill" process could be done under *any* conditions, not just calm ones.

(C) is irrelevant. The frequency of such ecological problems has no bearing on whether the author's proposal has merit or not.

(D) does not have to be true. Even if the tanks are drained and refilled at other times, it's still possible that they're only drained in port or near the coast. The author's proposal could still work by adding midocean refills.

Glossary

Logical Reasoning
Logical Reasoning Question Types

Argument-Based Questions

Main Point Question

A question that asks for an argument's conclusion or an author's main point. Typical question stems:

Which one the following most accurately expresses the conclusion of the argument as a whole?

Which one of the following sentences best expresses the main point of the scientist's argument?

Role of a Statement Question

A question that asks how a specific sentence, statement, or idea functions within an argument. Typical question stems:

Which one of the following most accurately describes the role played in the argument by the statement that automation within the steel industry allowed steel mills to produce more steel with fewer workers?

The claim that governmental transparency is a nation's primary defense against public-sector corruption figures in the argument in which one of the following ways?

Point at Issue Question

A question that asks you to identify the specific claim, statement, or recommendation about which two speakers/authors disagree (or, rarely, about which they agree). Typical question stems:

A point at issue between Tom and Jerry is

The dialogue most strongly supports the claim that Marilyn and Billy disagree with each other about which one of the following?

Method of Argument Question

A question that asks you to describe an author's argumentative strategy. In other words, the correct answer describes *how* the author argues (not necessarily what the author says). Typical question stems:

Which one of the following most accurately describes the technique of reasoning employed by the argument?

Julian's argument proceeds by

In the dialogue, Alexander responds to Abigail in which one of the following ways?

Parallel Reasoning Question

A question that asks you to identify the answer choice containing an argument that has the same logical structure and reaches the same type of conclusion as the argument in the stimulus does. Typical question stems:

The pattern of reasoning in which one of the following arguments is most parallel to that in the argument above?

The pattern of reasoning in which one of the following arguments is most similar to the pattern of reasoning in the argument above?

Assumption-Family Questions

Assumption Question

A question that asks you to identify one of the unstated premises in an author's argument. Assumption questions come in two varieties.

Necessary Assumption questions ask you to identify an unstated premise required for an argument's conclusion to follow logically from its evidence. Typical question stems:

Which one of the following is an assumption on which the argument depends?

Which one of the following is an assumption that the argument requires in order for its conclusion to be properly drawn?

Sufficient Assumption questions ask you to identify an unstated premise sufficient to establish the argument's conclusion on the basis of its evidence. Typical question stems:

The conclusion follows logically if which one of the following is assumed?

Which one of the following, if assumed, enables the conclusion above to be properly inferred?

Strengthen/Weaken Question

A question that asks you to identify a fact that, if true, would make the argument's conclusion more likely (Strengthen) or less likely (Weaken) to follow from its evidence. Typical question stems:

Strengthen

Which one of the following, if true, most strengthens the argument above?

Which one the following, if true, most strongly supports the claim above?

Weaken

Which one of the following, if true, would most weaken the argument above?

Which one of the following, if true, most calls into question the claim above?

Flaw Question

A question that asks you to describe the reasoning error that the author has made in an argument. Typical question stems:

The argument's reasoning is most vulnerable to criticism on the grounds that the argument

Which of the following identifies a reasoning error in the argument?

The reasoning in the correspondent's argument is questionable because the argument

Parallel Flaw Question

A question that asks you to identify the argument that contains the same error(s) in reasoning that the argument in the stimulus contains. Typical question stems:

The pattern of flawed reasoning exhibited by the argument above is most similar to that exhibited in which one of the following?

Which one of the following most closely parallels the questionable reasoning cited above?

Evaluate the Argument Question

A question that asks you to identify an issue or consideration relevant to the validity of an argument. Think of Evaluate questions as "Strengthen or Weaken" questions. The correct answer, if true, will strengthen the argument, and if false, will weaken the argument, or vice versa. Evaluate questions are very rare. Typical question stems:

Which one of the following would be most useful to know in order to evaluate the legitimacy of the professor's argument?

It would be most important to determine which one of the following in evaluating the argument?

Non-Argument Questions

Inference Question

A question that asks you to identify a statement that follows from the statements in the stimulus. It is very important to note the characteristics of the one correct and the four incorrect answers before evaluating the choices in Inference questions. Depending on the wording of the question stem, the correct answer to an Inference question may be the one that

- *must be true* if the statements in the stimulus are true

- is *most strongly supported* by the statements in the stimulus

- *must be false* if the statements in the stimulus are true

Typical question stems:

If all of the statements above are true, then which one of the following must also be true?

Which one of the following can be properly inferred from the information above?

If the statements above are true, then each of the following could be true EXCEPT:

Which one of the following is most strongly supported by the information above?

The statements above, if true, most support which one of the following?

The facts described above provide the strongest evidence against which one of the following?

Paradox Question

A question that asks you to identify a fact that, if true, most helps to explain, resolve, or reconcile an apparent contradiction. Typical question stems:

Which one of the following, if true, most helps to explain how both studies' findings could be accurate?

Which one the following, if true, most helps to resolve the apparent conflict in the spokesperson's statements?

Each one of the following, if true, would contribute to an explanation of the apparent discrepancy in the information above EXCEPT:

Principle Questions

Principle Question

A question that asks you to identify corresponding cases and principles. Some Principle questions provide a principle in the stimulus and call for the answer choice describing a case that corresponds to the principle. Others provide a specific case in the stimulus and call for the answer containing a principle to which that case corresponds.

On the LSAT, Principle questions almost always mirror the skills rewarded by other Logical Reasoning question types. After each of the following Principle question stems, we note the question type it resembles. Typical question stems:

Which one of the following principles, if valid, most helps to justify the reasoning above? (**Strengthen**)

Which one of the following most accurately expresses the principle underlying the reasoning above? (**Assumption**)

The situation described above most closely conforms to which of the following generalizations? (**Inference**)

Which one of the following situations conforms most closely to the principle described above? (**Inference**)

Which one of the following principles, if valid, most helps to reconcile the apparent conflict among the prosecutor's claims? (**Paradox**)

Parallel Principle Question

A question that asks you to identify a specific case that illustrates the same principle that is illustrated by the case described in the stimulus. Typical question stem:

Of the following, which one illustrates a principle that is most similar to the principle illustrated by the passage?

Untangling the Stimulus

Conclusion Types

The conclusions in arguments found in the Logical Reasoning section of the LSAT tend to fall into one of six categories:

1) Value Judgment (an evaluative statement; e.g., Action X is unethical, or Y's recital was poorly sung)

2) "If"/Then (a conditional prediction, recommendation, or assertion; e.g., If X is true, then so is Y, or If you an M, then you should do N)

3) Prediction (X *will* or *will not* happen in the future)

4) Comparison (X is taller/shorter/more common/less common, etc. than Y)

5) Assertion of Fact (X is true or X is false)

6) Recommendation (we *should* or *should not* do X)

One-Sentence Test

A tactic used to identify the author's conclusion in an argument. Consider which sentence in the argument is the one the author would keep if asked to get rid of everything except her main point.

Subsidiary Conclusion

A conclusion following from one piece of evidence and then used by the author to support his overall conclusion or main point. Consider the following argument:

> The pharmaceutical company's new experimental treatment did not succeed in clinical trials. As a result, the new treatment will not reach the market this year. Thus, the company will fall short of its revenue forecasts for the year.

Here, the sentence "As a result, the new treatment will not reach the market this year" is a subsidiary conclusion. It follows from the evidence that the new treatment failed in clinical trials, and it provides evidence for the overall conclusion that the company will not meet its revenue projections.

Keyword(s) in Logical Reasoning

A word or phrase that helps you untangle a question's stimulus by indicating the logical structure of the argument or the author's point. Here are three categories of Keywords to which LSAT experts pay special attention in Logical Reasoning:

Conclusion words; e.g., *therefore, thus, so, as a result, it follows that, consequently,* [evidence] *is evidence that* [conclusion]

Evidence word; e.g, *because, since, after all, for,* [evidence] *is evidence that* [conclusion]

Contrast words; e.g., *but, however, while, despite, in spite of, on the other hand* (These are especially useful in Paradox and Inference questions.)

Experts use Keywords even more extensively in Reading Comprehension. Learn the Keywords associated with the Reading Comprehension section, and apply them to Logical Reasoning when they are helpful.

Mismatched Concepts

One of two patterns to which authors' assumptions conform in LSAT arguments. Mismatched Concepts describes the assumption in arguments in which terms or concepts in the conclusion are different *in kind* from those in the evidence. The author assumes that there is a logical relationship between the different terms. For example:

> Bobby is a **championship swimmer**. Therefore, he **trains every day**.

Here, the words "trains every day" appear only in the conclusion, and the words "championship swimmer" appear only in the evidence. For the author to reach this conclusion from this evidence, he assumes that championship swimmers train every day.

Another example:

> Susan does **not eat her vegetables**. Thus, she will **not grow big and strong**.

In this argument, not growing big and strong is found only in the conclusion while not eating vegetables is found only in the evidence. For the author to reach this conclusion from this evidence, she must assume that eating one's vegetables is necessary for one to grow big and strong.

See also Overlooked Possibilities.

Overlooked Possibilities

One of two patterns to which authors' assumptions conform in LSAT arguments. Mismatched Concepts describes the assumption in arguments in which terms or concepts in the conclusion are different *in degree, scale, or level of certainty* from those in the evidence. The author assumes that there is no factor or explanation for the conclusion other than the one(s) offered in the evidence. For example:

> Samson does not have a ticket stub for this movie showing. Thus, Samson must have sneaked into the movie without paying.

The author assumes that there is no other explanation for Samson's lack of a ticket stub. The author overlooks several possibilities: e.g., Samson had a special pass for this showing of the movie; Samson dropped his ticket stub by accident or threw it away after entering the theater; someone else in Samson's party has all of the party members' ticket stubs in her pocket or handbag.

Another example:

> Jonah's marketing plan will save the company money. Therefore, the company should adopt Jonah's plan.

Here, the author makes a recommendation based on one advantage. The author assumes that the advantage is the company's only concern or that there are no disadvantages that could outweigh it, e.g., Jonah's plan might save money on marketing but not generate any new leads or customers; Jonah's plan might damage the company's image or reputation; Jonah's plan might include illegal false advertising. Whenever the author of an LSAT argument concludes with a recommendation or a prediction based on just a single fact in the evidence, that author is always overlooking many other possibilities.

See also Mismatched Concepts.

Causal Argument

An argument in which the author concludes or assumes that one thing causes another. The most common pattern on the LSAT is for the author to conclude that A causes B from evidence that A and B are correlated. For example:

> I notice that whenever the store has a poor sales month, employee tardiness is also higher that month. Therefore, it must be that employee tardiness causes the store to lose sales.

The author assumes that the correlation in the evidence indicates a causal relationship. These arguments are vulnerable to three types of overlooked possibilities:

1) There could be **another causal factor**. In the previous example, maybe the months in question are those in which the manager takes vacation, causing the store to lose sales and permitting employees to arrive late without fear of the boss's reprimands.

2) Causation could be **reversed**. Maybe in months when sales are down, employee morale suffers and tardiness increases as a result.

3) The correlation could be **coincidental**. Maybe the correlation between tardiness and the dip in sales is pure coincidence.

See also Flaw Types: Correlation versus Causation.

Another pattern in causal arguments (less frequent on the LSAT) involves the assumption that a particular causal mechanism is or is not involved in a causal relationship. For example:

> The airport has rerouted takeoffs and landings so that they will not create noise over the Sunnyside neighborhood. Thus, the recent drop in Sunnyside's property values cannot be explained by the neighborhood's proximity to the airport.

Here, the author assumes that the only way that the airport could be the cause of dropping property values is through noise pollution. The author overlooks any other possible mechanism (e.g., frequent traffic jams and congestion) through which proximity to the airport could be cause of Sunnyside's woes.

Principle

A broad, law-like rule, definition, or generalization that covers a variety of specific cases with defined attributes. To see how principles are treated on the LSAT, consider the following principle:

> It is immoral for a person for his own gain to mislead another person.

That principle would cover a specific case, such as a seller who lies about the quality of construction to get a higher price for his house. It would also correspond to the case of a teenager who, wishing to spend a night out on the town, tells his mom "I'm going over to Randy's house." He knows that his mom believes that he will be staying at Randy's house, when in fact, he and Randy will go out together.

That principle does not, however, cover cases in which someone lies solely for the purpose of making the other person feel better or in which one person inadvertently misleads the other through a mistake of fact.

Be careful not to apply your personal ethics or morals when analyzing the principles articulated on the test.

Flaw Types

Necessary versus Sufficient

This flaw occurs when a speaker or author concludes that one event is necessary for a second event from evidence that the first event is sufficient to bring about the second event, or vice versa. Example:

> If more than 25,000 users attempt to access the new app at the same time, the server will crash. Last night, at 11:15 pm, the server crashed, so it must be case that more than 25,000 users were attempting to use the new app at that time.

In making this argument, the author assumes that the only thing that will cause the server to crash is the usage level (i.e., high usage is *necessary* for the server to crash). The evidence, however, says that high usage is one thing that will cause the server to crash (i.e., that high usage is *sufficient* to crash the server).

Correlation versus Causation

This flaw occurs when a speaker or author draws a conclusion that one thing causes another from evidence that the two things are correlated. Example:

Over the past half century, global sugar consumption has tripled. That same time period has seen a surge in the rate of technological advancement worldwide. It follows that the increase in sugar consumption has caused the acceleration in technological advancement.

In any argument with this structure, the author is making three unwarranted assumptions. First, he assumes that there is no alternate cause, i.e., there is nothing else that has contributed to rapid technological advancement. Second, he assumes that the causation is not reversed, i.e., technological advancement has not contributed to the increase in sugar consumption, perhaps by making it easier to grow, refine, or transport sugar. And, third, he assumes that the two phenomena are not merely coincidental, i.e., that it is not just happenstance that global sugar consumption is up at the same time that the pace of technological advancement has accelerated.

Unrepresentative Sample

This flaw occurs when a speaker or author draws a conclusion about a group from evidence in which the sample cannot represent that group because the sample is too small or too selective, or is biased in some way. Example:

> Moviegoers in our town prefer action films and romantic comedies over other film genres. Last Friday, we sent reporters to survey moviegoers at several theaters in town, and nearly 90 percent of those surveyed were going to watch either an action film or a romantic comedy.

The author assumes that the survey was representative of the town's moviegoers, but there are several reasons to question that assumption. First, we don't know how many people were actually surveyed. Even if the number of people surveyed was adequate, we don't know how many other types of movies were playing. Finally, the author doesn't limit her conclusion to moviegoers on Friday nights. If the survey had been conducted at Sunday matinees, maybe most moviegoers would have been heading out to see an animated family film or a historical drama. Who knows?

Scope Shift/Unwarranted Assumption

This flaw occurs when a speaker's or author's evidence has a scope or has terms different enough from the scope or terms in his conclusion that it is doubtful that the evidence can support the conclusion. Example:

> A very small percentage of working adults in this country can correctly define collateralized debt obligation securities. Thus, sad to say, the majority of the nation's working adults cannot make prudent choices about how to invest their savings.

This speaker assumes that prudent investing requires the ability to accurately define a somewhat obscure financial term. But prudence is not the same thing as expertise, and the speaker does not offer any evidence that this knowledge of this particular term is related to wise investing.

Percent versus Number/Rate versus Number

This flaw occurs when a speaker or author draws a conclusion about real quantities from evidence about rates or percentages, or vice versa. Example:

> At the end of last season, Camp SunnyDay laid off half of their senior counselors and a quarter of their junior counselors. Thus, Camp SunnyDay must have more senior counselors than junior counselors.

The problem, of course, is that we don't know how many senior and junior counselors were on staff before the layoffs. If there were a total of 4 senior counselors and 20 junior counselors, then the camp would have laid off only 2 senior counselors while dismissing 5 junior counselors.

Equivocation

This flaw occurs when a speaker or author uses the same word in two different and incompatible ways. Example:

> Our opponent in the race has accused our candidate's staff members of behaving unprofessionally. But that's not fair. Our staff is made up entirely of volunteers, not paid campaign workers.

The speaker interprets the opponent's use of the word *professional* to mean "paid," but the opponent likely meant something more along the lines of "mature, competent, and businesslike."

Ad Hominem

This flaw occurs when a speaker or author concludes that another person's claim or argument is invalid because that other person has a personal flaw or shortcoming. One common pattern is for the speaker or author to claim the other person acts hypocritically or that the other person's claim is made from self-interest. Example:

> Mrs. Smithers testified before the city council, stating that the speed limits on the residential streets near her home are dangerously high. But why should we give her claim any credence? The way she eats and exercises, she's not even looking out for her own health.

The author attempts to undermine Mrs. Smithers's testimony by attacking her character and habits. He doesn't offer any evidence that is relevant to her claim about speed limits.

Part versus Whole

This flaw occurs when a speaker or author concludes that a part or individual has a certain characteristic because the whole or the larger group has that characteristic, or vice versa. Example:

> Patient: I should have no problems taking the three drugs prescribed to me by my doctors. I looked them up, and

none of the three is listed as having any major side effects.

Here, the patient is assuming that what is true of each of the drugs individually will be true of them when taken together. The patient's flaw is overlooking possible interactions that could cause problems not present when the drugs are taken separately.

Circular Reasoning

This flaw occurs when a speaker or author tries to prove a conclusion with evidence that is logically equivalent to the conclusion. Example:

> All those who run for office are prevaricators. To see this, just consider politicians: they all prevaricate.

Perhaps the author has tried to disguise the circular reasoning in this argument by exchanging the words "those who run for office" in the conclusion for "politicians" in the evidence, but all this argument amounts to is "Politicians prevaricate; therefore, politicians prevaricate." On the LSAT, circular reasoning is very rarely the correct answer to a Flaw question, although it is regularly described in one of the wrong answers.

Question Strategies

Denial Test

A tactic for identifying the assumption *necessary* to an argument. When you negate an assumption necessary to an argument, the argument will fall apart. Negating an assumption that is not necessary to the argument will not invalidate the argument. Consider the following argument:

> Only high schools which produced a state champion athlete during the school year will be represented at the Governor's awards banquet. Therefore, McMurtry High School will be represented at the Governor's awards banquet.

Which one of the following is an assumption necessary to that argument?

(1) McMurtry High School produced more state champion athletes than any other high school during the school year.

(2) McMurtry High School produced at least one state champion athlete during the school year.

If you are at all confused about which of those two statements reflects the *necessary* assumption, negate them both.

(1) McMurtry High School **did not produce more** state champion athletes than any other high school during the school year.

That does not invalidate the argument. McMurtry could still be represented at the Governor's banquet.

(2) McMurtry High School **did not produce any** state champion athletes during the school year.

Here, negating the statement causes the argument to fall apart. Statement (2) is an assumption *necessary* to the argument.

Point at Issue "Decision Tree"

A tactic for evaluating the answer choices in Point at Issue questions. The correct answer is the only answer choice to which you can answer "Yes" to all three questions in the following diagram.

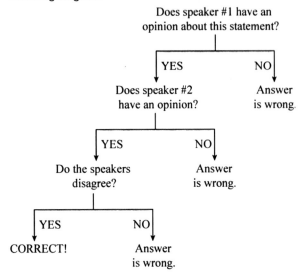

Common Methods of Argument

These methods of argument or argumentative strategies are common on the LSAT:

- Analogy, in which an author draws parallels between two unrelated (but purportedly similar) situations
- Example, in which an author cites a specific case or cases to justify a generalization
- Counterexample, in which an author seeks to discredit an opponent's argument by citing a specific case or cases that appear to invalidate the opponent's generalization
- Appeal to authority, in which an author cites an expert's claim or opinion as support for her conclusion
- Ad hominem attack, in which an author attacks her opponent's personal credibility rather than attacking the substance of her opponent's argument
- Elimination of alternatives, in which an author lists possibilities and discredits or rules out all but one

- Means/requirements, in which the author argues that something is needed to achieve a desired result

Wrong Answer Types in LR

Outside the Scope (Out of Scope; Beyond the Scope)

An answer choice containing a statement that is too broad, too narrow, or beyond the purview of the stimulus, making the statement in the choice irrelevant

180

An answer choice that directly contradicts what the correct answer must say (for example, a choice that strengthens the argument in a Weaken question)

Extreme

An answer choice containing language too emphatic to be supported by the stimulus; often (although not always) characterized by words such as *all*, *never*, *every*, *only*, or *most*

Distortion

An answer choice that mentions details from the stimulus but mangles or misstates what the author said about those details

Irrelevant Comparison

An answer choice that compares two items or attributes in a way not germane to the author's argument or statements

Half-Right/Half-Wrong

An answer choice that begins correctly, but then contradicts or distorts the passage in its second part; this wrong answer type is more common in Reading Comprehension than it is in Logical Reasoning

Faulty Use of Detail

An answer choice that accurately states something from the stimulus, but does so in a manner that answers the question incorrectly; this wrong answer type is more common in Reading Comprehension than it is in Logical Reasoning

Logic Games
Game Types

Strict Sequencing Game

A game that asks you to arrange entities into numbered positions or into a set schedule (usually hours or days). Strict Sequencing is, by far, the most common game type on the LSAT. In the typical Strict Sequencing game, there is a one-to-one matchup of entities and positions, e.g., seven entities to be placed in seven positions, one per position, or six entities to be placed over six consecutive days, one entity per day.

From time to time, the LSAT will offer Strict Sequencing with more entities than positions (e.g., seven entities to be arranged over five days, with some days to receive more than one entity) or more positions than entities (e.g., six entities to be scheduled over seven days, with at least one day to receive no entities).

Other, less common variations on Strict Sequencing include:

Double Sequencing, in which each entity is placed or scheduled two times (there have been rare occurrences of Triple or Quadruple Sequencing). Alternatively, a Double Sequencing game may involve two different sets of entities each sequenced once.

Circular Sequencing, in which entities are arranged around a table or in a circular arrangement (NOTE: When the positions in a Circular Sequencing game are numbered, the first and last positions are adjacent.)

Vertical Sequencing, in which the positions are numbered from top to bottom or from bottom to top (as in the floors of a building)

Loose Sequencing Game

A game that asks you to arrange or schedule entities in order but provides no numbering or naming of the positions. The rules in Loose Sequencing give only the relative positions (earlier or later, higher or lower) between two entities or among three entities. Loose Sequencing games almost always provide that there will be no ties between entities in the rank, order, or position they take.

Circular Sequencing Game

See Strict Sequencing Game.

Selection Game

A game that asks you to choose or include some entities from the initial list of entities and to reject or exclude others. Some Selection games provide overall limitations on the number of entities to be selected (e.g., "choose exactly four of seven students" or "choose at least two of six entrees") while others provide little or no restriction on the number selected ("choose at least one type of flower" or "select from among seven board members").

Distribution Game

A game that asks you to break up the initial list of entities into two, three, or (very rarely) four groups or teams. In the vast majority of Distribution games, each entity is assigned to one and only one group or team. A relatively common variation on Distribution games will provide a subdivided list of entities (e.g., eight students—four men and four women—will form three study groups) and will then require representatives from those subdivisions on each team (e.g., each study group will have at least one of the men on it).

Matching Game

A game that asks you to match one or more members of one set of entities to specific members of another set of entities, or that asks you to match attributes or objects to a set of entities. Unlike Distribution games, in which each entity is placed in exactly one group or team, Matching games usually permit you to assign the same attribute or object to more than one entity.

In some cases, there are overall limitations on the number of entities that can be matched (e.g., "In a school's wood shop, there are four workstations—numbered 1 through 4—and each workstation has at least one and at most three of the following tools—band saw, dremmel tool, electric sander, and power drill"). In almost all Matching games, further restrictions on the number of entities that can be matched to a particular person or place will be found in the rules (e.g., Workstation 4 will have more tools than Workstation 2 has).

Hybrid Game

A game that asks you to do two (or rarely, three) of the standard actions (Sequencing, Selection, Distribution, and Matching) to a set of entities.

The most common Hybrid is Sequencing-Matching. A typical Sequencing-Matching Hybrid game might ask you to schedule six speakers at a conference to six one-hour speaking slots (from 9 am to 2 pm), and then assign each speaker one of two subjects (economic development or trade policy).

Nearly as common as Sequencing-Matching is Distribution-Sequencing. A typical game of this type might ask you to divide six people in a talent competition into either a Dance category or a Singing category, and then rank the competitors in each category.

It is most common to see one Hybrid game in each Logic Games section, although there have been tests with two Hybrid games and tests with none. To determine the type of Hybrid you are faced with, identify the game's action in Step 1 of the Logic Games Method. For example, a game asking you to choose four of six runners, and then assign the four chosen runners to lanes numbered 1 through 4 on a track, would be a Selection-Sequencing Hybrid game.

Mapping Game

A game that provides you with a description of geographical locations and, typically, of the connections among them. Mapping games often ask you to determine the shortest possible routes between two locations or to account for the number of connections required to travel from one location to another. This game type is extremely rare, and as of February 2017, a Mapping game was last seen on PrepTest 40 administered in June 2003.

Process Game

A game that opens with an initial arrangement of entities (e.g., a starting sequence or grouping) and provides rules that describe the processes through which that arrangement can be altered. The questions typically ask you for acceptable arrangements or placements of particular entities after one, two, or three stages in the process. Occasionally, a Process game question might provide information about the arrangement after one, two, or three stages in the process and ask you what must have happened in the earlier stages. This game type is extremely rare, and as of November 2016, a Process game was last seen on PrepTest 16 administered in September 1995. However, there was a Process game on PrepTest 80, administered in December 2016, thus ending a 20-year hiatus.

Game Setups and Deductions

Floater

An entity that is not restricted by any rule or limitation in the game

Blocks of Entities

Two or more entities that are required by rule to be adjacent or separated by a set number of spaces (Sequencing games), to be placed together in the same group (Distribution games), to be matched to the same entity (Matching games), or to be selected or rejected together (Selection games)

Limited Options

Rules or restrictions that force all of a game's acceptable arrangements into two (or occasionally three) patterns

Established Entities

An entity required by rule to be placed in one space or assigned to one particular group throughout the entire game

Number Restrictions

Rules or limitations affecting the number of entities that may be placed into a group or space throughout the game

Duplications

Two or more rules that restrict a common entity. Usually, these rules can be combined to reach additional deductions. For example, if you know that B is placed earlier than A in a sequence and that C is placed earlier than B in that sequence, you can deduce that C is placed earlier than A in the sequence and that there is at least one space (the space occupied by B) between C and A.

Master Sketch

The final sketch derived from the game's setup, rules, and deductions. LSAT experts preserve the Master Sketch for reference as they work through the questions. The Master

Sketch does not include any conditions from New-"If" question stems.

Logic Games Question Types

Acceptability Question

A question in which the correct answer is an acceptable arrangement of all the entities relative to the spaces, groups, or selection criteria in the game. Answer these by using the rules to eliminate answer choices that violate the rules.

Partial Acceptability Question

A question in which the correct answer is an acceptable arrangement of some of the entities relative to some of the spaces, groups, or selection criteria in the game, and in which the arrangement of entities not included in the answer choices could be acceptable to the spaces, groups, or selection criteria not explicitly shown in the answer choices. Answer these the same way you would answer Acceptability questions, by using the rules to eliminate answer choices that explicitly or implicitly violate the rules.

Must Be True/False; Could Be True/False Question

A question in which the correct answer must be true, could be true, could be false, or must be false (depending on the question stem), and in which no additional rules or conditions are provided by the question stem

New-"If" Question

A question in which the stem provides an additional rule, condition, or restriction (applicable only to that question), and then asks what must/could be true/false as a result. LSAT experts typically handle New-"If" questions by copying the Master Sketch, adding the new restriction to the copy, and working out any additional deductions available as a result of the new restriction before evaluating the answer choices.

Rule Substitution Question

A question in which the correct answer is a rule that would have an impact identical to one of the game's original rules on the entities in the game

Rule Change Question

A question in which the stem alters one of the original rules in the game, and then asks what must/could be true/false as a result. LSAT experts typically handle Rule Change questions by reconstructing the game's sketch, but now accounting for the changed rule in place of the original. These questions are rare on recent tests.

Rule Suspension Question

A question in which the stem indicates that you should ignore one of the original rules in the game, and then asks what must/could be true/false as a result. LSAT experts typically handle Rule Suspension questions by reconstructing the game's sketch, but now accounting for the absent rule. These questions are very rare.

Complete and Accurate List Question

A question in which the correct answer is a list of any and all entities that could acceptably appear in a particular space or group, or a list of any and all spaces or groups in which a particular entity could appear

Completely Determine Question

A question in which the correct answer is a condition that would result in exactly one acceptable arrangement for all of the entities in the game

Supply the "If" Question

A question in which the correct answer is a condition that would guarantee a particular result stipulated in the question stem

Minimum/Maximum Question

A question in which the correct answer is the number corresponding to the fewest or greatest number of entities that could be selected (Selection), placed into a particular group (Distribution), or matched to a particular entity (Matching). Often, Minimum/Maximum questions begin with New-"If" conditions.

Earliest/Latest Question

A question in which the correct answer is the earliest or latest position in which an entity may acceptably be placed. Often, Earliest/Latest questions begin with New-"If" conditions.

"How Many" Question

A question in which the correct answer is the exact number of entities that may acceptably be placed into a particular group or space. Often, "How Many" questions begin with New-"If" conditions.

Reading Comprehension
Strategic Reading

Roadmap

The test taker's markup of the passage text in Step 1 (Read the Passage Strategically) of the Reading Comprehension Method. To create helpful Roadmaps, LSAT experts circle or underline Keywords in the passage text and jot down brief, helpful notes or paragraph summaries in the margin of their test booklets.

Keyword(s) in Reading Comprehension

Words in the passage text that reveal the passage structure or the author's point of view and thus help test takers anticipate and research the questions that accompany the passage. LSAT experts pay attention to six categories of Keywords in Reading Comprehension:

Emphasis/Opinion—words that signal that the author finds a detail noteworthy or that the author has positive or negative opinion about a detail; any subjective or evaluative language on the author's part (e.g., *especially, crucial, unfortunately, disappointing, I suggest, it seems likely*)

Contrast—words indicating that the author finds two details or ideas incompatible or that the two details illustrate conflicting points (e.g., *but, yet, despite, on the other hand*)

Logic—words that indicate an argument, either the author's or someone else's (e.g., *thus, therefore, because, it follows that*)

Illustration—words indicating an example offered to clarify or support another point (e.g., *for example, this shows, to illustrate*)

Sequence/Chronology—words showing steps in a process or developments over time (e.g., *traditionally, in the past, today, first, second, finally, earlier, subsequent*)

Continuation—words indicating that a subsequent example or detail supports the same point or illustrates the same idea as the previous example (e.g., *moreover, in addition, also, further, along the same lines*)

Margin Notes

The brief notes or paragraph summaries that the test taker jots down next to the passage in the margin of the test booklet

Big Picture Summaries: Topic/Scope/Purpose/Main Idea

A test taker's mental summary of the passage as a whole made during Step 1 (Read the Passage Strategically) of the Reading Comprehension Method. LSAT experts account for four aspects of the passage in their big picture summaries:

Topic—the overall subject of the passage

Scope—the particular aspect of the Topic that the author focuses on

Purpose—the author's reason or motive for writing the passage (express this as a verb; e.g., *to refute, to outline, to evaluate, to critique*)

Main Idea—the author's conclusion or overall takeaway; if the passage does not contain an explicit conclusion or thesis, you can combine the author's Scope and Purpose to get a good sense of the Main Idea.

Passage Types

Kaplan categorizes Reading Comprehension passages in two ways, by subject matter and by passage structure.

Subject matter categories

In the majority of LSAT Reading Comprehension sections, there is one passage from each of the following subject matter categories:

Humanities—topics from art, music, literature, philosophy, etc.

Natural Science—topics from biology, astronomy, paleontology, physics, etc.

Social Science—topics from anthropology, history, sociology, psychology, etc.

Law—topics from constitutional law, international law, legal education, jurisprudence, etc.

Passage structure categories

The majority of LSAT Reading Comprehension passages correspond to one of the following descriptions. The first categories—Theory/Perspective and Event/Phenomenon—have been the most common on recent LSATs.

Theory/Perspective—The passage focuses on a thinker's theory or perspective on some aspect of the Topic; typically (though not always), the author disagrees and critiques the thinker's perspective and/or defends his own perspective.

Event/Phenomenon—The passage focuses on an event, a breakthrough development, or a problem that has recently arisen; when a solution to the problem is proposed, the author most often agrees with the solution (and that represents the passage's Main Idea).

Biography—The passage discusses something about a notable person; the aspect of the person's life emphasized by the author reflects the Scope of the passage.

Debate—The passage outlines two opposing positions (neither of which is the author's) on some aspect of the Topic; the author may side with one of the positions, may remain neutral, or may critique both. (This structure has been relatively rare on recent LSATs.)

Comparative Reading

A pair of passages (labeled Passage A and Passage B) that stand in place of the typical single passage exactly one time in each Reading Comprehension section administered since June 2007. The paired Comparative Reading passages share the same Topic, but may have different Scopes and Purposes. On most LSAT tests, a majority of the questions accompanying Comparative Reading passages require the test taker to compare or contrast ideas or details from both passages.

Question Strategies

Research Clues

A reference in a Reading Comprehension question stem to a word, phrase, or detail in the passage text, or to a particular line number or paragraph in the passage. LSAT experts recognize five kinds of research clues:

Line Reference—An LSAT expert researches around the referenced lines, looking for Keywords that indicate why the referenced details were included or how they were used by the author.

Paragraph Reference—An LSAT expert consults her passage Roadmap to see the paragraph's Scope and Purpose.

Quoted Text (often accompanied by a line reference)—An LSAT expert checks the context of the quoted term or phrase, asking what the author meant by it in the passage.

Proper Nouns—An LSAT expert checks the context of the person, place, or thing in the passage, asking whether the author made a positive, negative, or neutral evaluation of it and why the author included it in the passage.

Content Clues—These are terms, concepts, or ideas from the passage mentioned in the question stem but not as direct quotes and not accompanied by line references. An LSAT expert knows that content clues almost always refer to something that the author emphasized or about which the author expressed an opinion.

Reading Comp Question Types

Global Question

A question that asks for the Main Idea of the passage or for the author's primary Purpose in writing the passage. Typical question stems:

> Which one of the following most accurately expresses the main point of the passage?

> The primary purpose of the passage is to

Detail Question

A question that asks what the passage explicitly states about a detail. Typical question stems:

> According to the passage, some critics have criticized Gilliam's films on the grounds that

> The passage states that one role of a municipality's comptroller in budget decisions by the city council is to

> The author identifies which one of the following as a commonly held but false preconception?

> The passage contains sufficient information to answer which of the following questions?

Occasionally, the test will ask for a correct answer that contains a detail *not* stated in the passage:

> The author attributes each of the following positions to the Federalists EXCEPT:

Inference Question

A question that asks for a statement that follows from or is based on the passage but that is not necessarily stated explicitly in the passage. Some Inference questions contain research clues. The following are typical Inference question stems containing research clues:

> Based on the passage, the author would be most likely to agree with which one of the following statements about unified field theory?

> The passage suggests which one of the following about the behavior of migratory water fowl?

> Given the information in the passage, to which one of the following would radiocarbon dating techniques likely be applicable?

Other Inference questions lack research clues in the question stem. They may be evaluated using the test taker's Big Picture Summaries, or the answer choices may make it clear that the test taker should research a particular part of the passage text. The following are typical Inference question stems containing research clues:

> It can be inferred from the passage that the author would be most likely to agree that

> Which one of the following statements is most strongly supported by the passage?

Other Reading Comprehension question types categorized as Inference questions are Author's Attitude questions and Vocabulary-in-Context questions.

Logic Function Question

A question that asks why the author included a particular detail or reference in the passage or how the author used a particular detail or reference. Typical question stems:

> The author of the passage mentions declining inner-city populations in the paragraph most likely in order to

> The author's discussion of Rimbaud's travels in the Mediterranean (lines 23–28) functions primarily to

> Which one of the following best expresses the function of the third paragraph in the passage?

Logic Reasoning Question

A question that asks the test taker to apply Logical Reasoning skills in relation to a Reading Comprehension passage. Logic Reasoning questions often mirror Strengthen or Parallel Reasoning questions, and occasionally mirror Method of Argument or Principle questions. Typical question stems:

> Which one of the following, if true, would most strengthen the claim made by the author in the last sentence of the passage (lines 51–55)?

> Which one of the following pairs of proposals is most closely analogous to the pair of studies discussed in the passage?

Author's Attitude Question

A question that asks for the author's opinion or point of view on the subject discussed in the passage or on a detail mentioned in the passage. Since the correct answer may follow from the passage without being explicitly stated in it, some Author's Attitude questions are characterized as a subset of Inference questions. Typical question stems:

> The author's attitude toward the use of DNA evidence in the appeals by convicted felons is most accurately described as
>
> The author's stance regarding monetarist economic theories can most accurately be described as one of

Vocabulary-in-Context Question

A question that asks how the author uses a word or phrase within the context of the passage. The word or phrase in question is always one with multiple meanings. Since the correct answer follows from its use in the passage, Vocabulary-in-Context questions are characterized as a subset of Inference questions. Typical question stems:

> Which one of the following is closest in meaning to the word "citation" as it used in the second paragraph of the passage (line 18)?
>
> In context, the word "enlightenment" (line 24) refers to

Wrong Answer Types in RC

Outside the Scope (Out of Scope; Beyond the Scope)

An answer choice containing a statement that is too broad, too narrow, or beyond the purview of the passage

180

An answer choice that directly contradicts what the correct answer must say

Extreme

An answer choice containing language too emphatic (e.g., *all, never, every, none*) to be supported by the passage

Distortion

An answer choice that mentions details or ideas from the passage but mangles or misstates what the author said about those details or ideas

Faulty Use of Detail

An answer choice that accurately states something from the passage but in a manner that incorrectly answers the question

Half-Right/Half-Wrong

An answer choice in which one clause follows from the passage while another clause contradicts or deviates from the passage

Formal Logic Terms

Conditional Statement ("If"-Then Statement)

A statement containing a sufficient clause and a necessary clause. Conditional statements can be described in Formal Logic shorthand as:

> If [sufficient clause]　→ [necessary clause]

In some explanations, the LSAT expert may refer to the sufficient clause as the statement's "trigger" and to the necessary clause as the statement's result.

For more on how to interpret, describe, and use conditional statements on the LSAT, please refer to "A Note About Formal Logic on the LSAT" in this book's introduction.

Contrapositive

The conditional statement logically equivalent to another conditional statement formed by reversing the order of and negating the terms in the original conditional statement. For example, reversing and negating the terms in this statement:

> *If*　　*A*　　　　　　　→　　　　*B*

results in its contrapositive:

> *If*　　~*B*　　　　　　→　　　　~*A*

To form the contrapositive of conditional statements in which either the sufficient clause or the necessary clause has more than one term, you must also change the conjunction *and* to *or*, or vice versa. For example, reversing and negating the terms and changing *and* to *or* in this statement:

> *If*　　*M*　　　　　　→　　　　*O AND P*

results in its contrapositive:

> *If*　　~*O OR* ~*P*　　　→　　　　~*M*

CPSIA information can be obtained
at www.ICGtesting.com
Printed in the USA
LVOW09s0417270717
542801LV00028B/591/P

9 781506 223353